2-

Twelfth Man
in the
Huddle

Twelfth Man in the Huddle

David L. Diles

Word Books, Publisher
Waco, Texas

TWELFTH MAN IN THE HUDDLE

ISBN 0-87680-442-3

Library of Congress catalog card number: 76-19529

To Evelyn

Contents

Foreword

One of the thrilling spiritual stories today is the way God has been at work in the lives of many professional athletes. I am thankful that Dave Diles in this book has given us an exciting insight into the spiritual struggles and triumphs of many of football's top professional players. Men whose names are familiar across America are seen in a new light, as we discover their backgrounds and share in their common commitment to Christ.

To many, the life of a professional football player seems to be all glamour and excitement. In this book, however, we see the hard work, the tensions, and the disappointments which are part of the everyday life of the pro player. In a fresh way we see also that fame, money, and success do not necessarily bring happiness and meaning to life. God has created each of us for a purpose, and until we find and follow God's purpose for our lives we will never know the full peace and joy which Christ promised. This is as true for the football player as it is for the football spectator. Only Christ can give us true meaning in life, as we commit ourselves to him.

Many professional football players have discovered this, and are seeking to live for Christ. May God use their example, as seen in this book, to bring others to himself.

BILLY GRAHAM

Preface

In the often-times overblown and super-magnified world of professional sports, we sometimes lose sight of the fact that under the padded and decorated façade lives a man much like the rest of us—subject to the same stresses, uncertainties, frustrations, disappointments, and searching for more than what sports can give him.

Dave Diles, the newsman from his earliest days, has been able to probe through and beneath the façade to find that person. Dave Diles the man does it even better.

There are many things about *Twelfth Man in the Huddle* that would cause me to praise it. The chapter with Merlin Olsen is a sermon in itself. This is a book by a man about men. It deserves to be read.

PETE ROZELLE
Commissioner, NFL

Introduction

The inspiration for this book has come from many people over many seasons of life.

It came first from God-fearing parents who lived their sermons, who had so much goodness in their hearts and love in their home that five sometimes-tattered children never knew they were poor. They were not so priggish, these nice folks, that they could not enjoy good humor and not so pious that they could not tolerate human frailty.

My father taught me that it was not only possible, but wise, to be masculine and a Christian at the same time. He disdained those who sentimentalized Jesus as some limp-wristed, almost effeminate character. Surely he was gracious and kind and gentle at times, and always forgiving and understanding and compassionate—but it was Jesus who drove the money-changers from the temple. Lisle Desmond Diles always hit hard on the verb "drove" and enjoyed embellishing the point by cautioning, "The Book doesn't say Christ *asked* the money-changers to leave the temple, and it doesn't say he *negotiated* with them to get out."

The Jesus Christ my father knew best is a strong, virile, implacable man of abundant strength and courage. His reasoning was simple and sound: Could any other kind of man have drawn other men to him as Christ did? Could one of faltering courage go to the cross?

The Jesus Christ my father knew was first Lord and Savior, but he was human, too, and perhaps that is why they knew each other so well. My father could not ignore the fact that Christ had been tempted nor the fact that just before he was crucified, he asked that the cup be passed from him, and that during his final moments of agony, he cried out "My God, My God, why hast Thou forsaken me?"

These things, to my father, represented the human side of the One who wants to be the Savior of us all.

Doesn't the awareness of these things make him a more personal, a more human, a more believable Lord?

Lucille Bowman Diles could not have lived with more than thirty years of pain and suffering without a working, daily relationship with God. He gave her the strength and tolerance to

13

endure all, and the beautiful skills to write about her long illness:

> In the glorious Hereafter when the veil is swept away,
> I will know with perfect knowledge what I marvel at
> today,
> I will know why came the tempest to my sunny skies
> so soon,
> And why my sweetest blossoms were faded, ere the
> noon.

Theirs was not a blind and stubborn faith in an unknown God. They knew him quite well, thank you, and if you didn't, it was like not being able to smell a flower or see the sunrise.

One of the more frequently written lines is that young people are constantly amazed at how intelligent their parents get as the children grow older. At fourteen, I could not comprehend why a nice, Christian lady had to suffer the agonies of death and lie on a bed of pain, while those I thought of as non-Christian seemed to be getting a better shake out of life.

The question to her, obviously, was "Where is this kind and loving and gracious and understanding God of yours now?"

Her answer was predictably simple: "He is in heaven, where he always is. And he knows, even better than I, how much I can take, and how heavy a burden I can bear. He'll never give one of his own more of a cross than he can carry, with His help."

And the lady was smiling all the while!

It was at about that time in my life that Uncle Jim and Aunt Jessie Hundley came home from Africa to retire. They had been missionaries for more than twenty-five years to a land Uncle Jim always liked to call "deepest and darkest Africa."

We were American Baptists; my uncle and aunt were Nazarenes. They never had children of their own but they counted as their very own "all those little natives who came to us full of fear and apprehension, and to whom we gave the English language, then the Word of God."

They came often for dinner, and in the forties when lots of things were in short supply, we children sat without murmuring as Uncle Jim piled three and four heaping teaspoons of sugar into a single cup of coffee. We were under strict orders never to put more than a single teaspoon on our cereal, and when Uncle Jim would begin that seemingly-endless transporting of precious sugar from bowl to cup we'd sneak a glance at each other and cringe silently.

That, my friend, is a blend of Christian tolerance and a home whose members understood well the chain of command.

Aunt Jessie had never enjoyed very good health, and when her time came, they were living in a rented house next door.

It was a muggy Sunday afternoon and the oppressive heat and humidity had so enveloped the little town of Middleport, Ohio, that even the dogs could not budge from their yards. Nothing stirred. Uncle Jim and my mother had taken turns putting cold cloths on Aunt Jessie's forehead, and trying to stir some air with some of those old fans from the Rawlings & Coats Funeral Home. She was conscious to the end, and I was standing at the foot of her bed when Uncle Jim asked her "Jessie, do you want anything else?"

"Yes," she said in a barely audible whisper. "Heaven."

It was the first time I had seen anybody die.

Uncle Jim turned his sweaty, old gray head toward my mother then reached for her hand. She was crying, but softly.

They embraced, and Uncle Jim and my mother cried together. He was a big, strong man whose muscles were still well-toned despite the years. I saw his shoulders tremble as the two of them tried to comfort each other. Then my mother turned to me, took me by the hand, and the three of us walked onto the long front porch shaded from the blistering sun.

There, on that porch on Beech Street, the two of them talked with a teen-ager about death, and Uncle Jim quoted the passage I was to hear paraphrased a hundred times in song in the First Baptist Church—the part about "Death, where is thy sting? Grave, where is thy victory?"

I'm certain I never saw my father cry until the day Mom died. It was on Valentine's Day 1964 and perhaps it is no more than an eerie coincidence but that day was World Day of Prayer, and in addition to being the day set aside for love, it was the fiftieth anniversary of her baptism in the church.

All five kids had come to think of my father as a sort of Gibraltar, an imperturbable giant who knew sorrow but never tears. He was the dispenser of comfort and the easer of pain, the source of understanding and wisdom. Not that mother wasn't, but he was strong and stern and mainly silent, although not without great humor at times. It was the dry, English kind, laced with occasional bits of cynicism and sarcasm. She was flighty and more lenient, a Good Samaritan who might forget to fix your lunch when you came home from school but who, the same morning, had not forgotten to fix a huge kettle of soup for the folks down the street who had less than we did.

She fell ill on a Thursday and I got the call in Detroit. Dad said she had passed the first crisis and that I should wait until Friday evening before driving home. To rush there on Thursday, he reasoned, might frighten her into thinking her condition was terribly dire. No one ever questioned his reasoning and she died on Friday before I got home.

The nurses and Dr. Raymond Boice told us how she went. She had been doing a little missionary work, that's all, telling the doctor he should be more involved in church. After all, doctors see life coming in and going out and they're witnesses to more miracles than most of us. If any group should believe in him and his works, it seemed only natural it'd be the medical folks. With that, she slipped away.

The day after the funeral, before beginning the long drive back to Detroit, I sought my father out in their bedroom.

She was in heaven, I knew, but I wanted to know all that he knew about heaven. Where is it, what is it, what's it like, and so on.

"I don't know a whole lot about it," said the man who for years had been a deacon and a Sunday school teacher and a Bible student. He quoted the passage from First Corinthians about "Eye hath not seen, nor ear heard, neither have entered into the heart of man, the things which God hath prepared for them that love him." Beyond that, he said he didn't fully understand a lot of the things in the Bible, particularly the Book of Revelation. He was quick to add that he didn't really understand preachers who claimed to know all the mysteries of Revelation, and he reckoned there were just some things that God didn't figure the average man had enough sense to comprehend.

"All I know about heaven," he concluded, "is that whatever it is, and wherever it is, it's a whole lot better than this, and I want to go there."

Somewhere years ago I read a beautiful piece of poetry by Edmund Vance Cooke and these are the last four lines of it:

Death comes with a crawl or comes with a pounce,
And whether he's slow or spry,

It isn't the fact that you're dead that counts,
But only how did you die?

Mother had died, with the blessed assurance that we sing of, and she died trying to introduce others to her Savior.

Dad began to die then. Odd, but he had never really looked tired before. He was so robust, always 200 pounds in the cold weather and 190 in the hot. He was six feet one, broad-shouldered and strong with perfect posture, and none of us kids can remember him ever taking a day off work from his job as a freight conductor for the New York Central because of sickness. He told me he never had headaches, never even had a cavity. I suppose he never really had time for those things.

The ground rules had been laid out years before, but in case anyone needed a refresher course he gave the word just after Mom died. The kids suggested that he come and live with one of us. After all, the house was big, and there were those memories all around.

"The memories are in the heart," he had said, "not in the home."

That took care of that and there was no more talk of him moving.

Funny, how certain little things that people do or say stick with you. Every once in a while I recall an incident at Mom's funeral. Just before the services, Mrs. William Winston waddled up to the casket to pay her respects. The Winston family was black, but prejudice has to be taught and it wasn't taught at our house.

She was about as wide as she was tall and her squat body shook all over as she wiped away the tears and said to me, "If that little lady doesn't have a high seat in heaven, then the rest of us might as well jes' quit."

I think that's pretty much what Dad did. He didn't quit believing, he didn't quit praying; he just quit caring about living. I had taken a private plane to be at his bedside just a few hours after he suffered his massive heart attack. He was awake and he made good sense. Very good sense, in fact.

When I talked of his getting up and around and out of the hospital before long, he shook his head.

"I really don't want any part of that," he said. "This may be difficult for you to understand, and I don't mean to sound maudlin, but I'd much prefer just to die. I have five healthy children and nice grandchildren. I'm seventy-seven years old and I've been all the places I'm going to go and done all the things I'm going to do. I anticipate just one thing now, and that is going to heaven to be with Mother."

Now you tell me: How does the baby of five children, a man of not-quite-thirty-five, challenge that kind of authority or question that kind of logic?

He got his wish, never leaving the little hospital in the neighboring village of Pomeroy. One of the nurses said that moments before he went to sleep for the last time, he had asked her to hand him his billfold from the dresser drawer. They had been talking about work and hard times and there never seeming to be enough money to go around these days.

Dad reached inside his wallet and extracted a verse of Scripture sealed inside a little piece of plastic. He had carried it with him for years and it was Philippians 4:11: "Not that I speak in respect of want, for I have learned, in whatsoever state I am, therewith to be content."

The rewards he and Mom reaped were never the financial, tangible kind. But they had riches untold—like the songwriter said—and every time I hear or read of some jet-setter flitting about, trying to find new ways to spend millions to find a so-called secret of life, I think of my Mom and my Dad. And I think, too, of a quotation she sent me years ago, "It is not he who has little who is poor, rather he who constantly wants more."

The only thing they really wanted, they got.

Along the way, there have been many other people whose lives have touched mine who've served as inspirations for this book. One would be the late Forrest Bachtel, my high school coach. He had been a Little All-American football performer, yet he managed to combine these great athletic skills and teaching abilities with Christian conduct. And when death came to him, after long years of suffering, he took it like a man totally prepared, even anxious, to meet his Maker.

Harold Wetherholt gave me a job as a full-time reporter on the *Gallipolis Tribune* and *Gallia Times* when I was a shaver of fourteen, and taught me the art of plain talk.

John Pival persuaded me to get into television and taught me the true meaning of mass media communication. It was a simple thing, really. His theory was that "masses" figures out to a whole lot of folks. "Media" was just the method by which we got the message across. And "communication" was what we were trying to do.

The Reverend Howard Eicher just may be the finest man I've ever met in the ministry of Jesus Christ. He's a man who speaks the truth and can stand to hear it. I've never pulled any punches with him, and he still loves me. That's very nice, considering that he knows all the bad things about me.

Not to be overlooked, in considering the people who inspired the writing of this book, are television fans around the country.

In nearly thirty years of communications, there have been literally thousands of speeches before every conceivable type of audience. Invariably, when there was a question-and-answer session following the speech, some gritty soul would ask, "Why don't you fellows in television ever report any good news?"

The answer was typically journalistic, explaining that departure from what is considered normal behavior creates news. One who refuses to sign a contract makes a bigger story than those who do—because it's fairly normal, or it used to be anyway— for an athlete to sign a contract. The player whose off-the-field escapades draw the attention of policemen finds himself off the sports pages and onto the front.

Some folks, I'm certain, never quite understood the reply nor cared for it. Sometimes it pained me that the explanation of "news" was inadequate.

This, then, is to satisfy them, Lisle and Lucille Diles, and countless others who have given so much that is so good for so long, and who have longed only for good news about good people who go about trying to do good things.

DAVE DILES

1

The Man Who Has Almost Everything

Practice was over and the quarterback had come straight home. He slumped down into a comfortable chair, but there was no comfort to be found.

He had been knocked out of his job as the number one quarterback. A bad marriage was behind him, but the taste of it lingered and brought bitterness. He had his fill of the groupies and camp followers. Down deep, they were shallow.

He had tried drinking with the boys and hitting every pub in town, but he wasn't a very good drinker. Besides, honky-tonkin' was alien to the way he was reared.

He had been booed lustily by the fans and ripped apart unmercifully by the news media. His critics were loud and great in number, and they questioned not only his abilities but his intelligence.

The strong faith that nurtured him since childhood was on the shelf and he was on the bench. He did not have a single friend to whom he could turn with total candor and expect full understanding. Sympathy, yes. But he had quite enough of that for himself.

Finally, Terry Bradshaw of the Pittsburgh Steelers quit trying to solve his problems by himself. He closed his eyes, put his head in his hands and began to cry. Then he spoke aloud: "Here I am, God. I've tried to handle it all by myself, and I just can't get the job done. So I'm placing my life in your hands. I need some peace of mind, and I know you can give it to me. From this minute on, you're the boss. You're number one."

Terry Bradshaw never left his comfortable apartment that night. After praying for a long time, he felt the weight of the world had been lifted from his generous shoulders—shoulders strong enough to absorb the punishment of rugged defensive players in the National Football League, but too weak to handle the problems that beset him off the field.

The following day he returned to the practice field and was smiling. He spoke to his teammates, took his place with the second stringers, never once questioned the judgment of coach Chuck Noll, and felt magnificent.

"I had been nothing but turmoil," he said. "I was a volcano inside. My problems were destroying me. For four years I had separated myself from God. I was not the Christian I should have been, but God never once left me. I had just put myself out of touch with him and had lived only for myself.

"But when I turned the controls back to God, I knew that I had the capacity to accept whatever might come. If success came, I knew I'd be able to handle that. And if adversity continued, I knew he'd ride out the storms with me."

All that took place in October 1974. The following week Bradshaw was again the starting quarterback—later was benched again—and still later came back to get the top job once more. It was Bradshaw who quarterbacked the Pittsburgh Steelers to victory in the Super Bowl in January 1975.

There were remarkable changes in October and Terry was acutely aware of every one of them. "I was very much content with anything and everything. I wanted to win and I prepared to win, but I knew I could accept setbacks if they came. I knew I could accept victory and not be overwhelmed by it, and I knew I could accept defeat as a challenge from God. I'd lost all confidence in myself and seriously considered quitting pro ball, but all of a sudden I had poise, confidence, and maturity."

It was that poise, confidence, and maturity that carried the Steelers to their first conference championship in forty-two years—a 24–13 achievement over the Oakland Raiders—and a 16–6 triumph over the Minnesota Vikings in the Super Bowl.

As soon as that game was over Bradshaw met the press in the Steelers' locker room. There, he told of the turnaround in his personal life, his new relationship with Jesus Christ, and his commitment to God. The team's chaplain had encouraged Terry to speak out publicly when the Steelers beat the Buffalo Bills for the American Conference title. The chaplain was sure the Oakland victory would prompt Bradshaw to tell the world of his newfound faith. But for Bradshaw, the Super Bowl was the only appropriate occasion.

"I really never got a great charge out of winning the Super Bowl. I enjoyed it and I wanted to win, but it didn't give me a great personal lift. I didn't feel vindicated or anything else because I had confidence in myself and my own destiny, and I wasn't really concerned over what was written or said about me. All that matters is what God thinks of me.

"But I had made a promise to God. He never let me down, and I knew this would be one tremendous opportunity to publicly confess my faith in God. He has commanded us to do that, you know. I'm so proud that God loves me, and that I love him, so I felt obliged to say it where I could reach the most people."

Hardly anyone knew about it when a ten-year-old Terry Bradshaw first publicly confessed his faith in Jesus. Bill and Novis Bradshaw are God-fearing, Bible-reading Baptists, and the family was in church every time the doors were opened. That meant Sunday school, church, and evening services each Sunday, plus prayer meetings on Wednesday nights. The three Bradshaw boys had youth meetings on Sunday evenings as well. Bill Bradshaw long has been a deacon in the church, and he and his wife made certain that Bible study and family prayer were a part of their daily lives.

They tried to make faith a simple thing for their children. As a youngster, Terry was taught simple messages about Jesus Christ—that he was born the son of God, that he lived on earth, that he died on the cross for the remission of the sins of all men, that he rose again, and that he will come again.

"They let us learn about God in an uncomplicated way," Terry recalled. "I think the main thing was keeping us in church and giving us Christian surroundings. You know, even today I realize that you have to be around Christian people in order to really grow as a Christian. If you're not around good folks, you can lose the feel. My parents never really pushed us. Instead, they just let us absorb as much as we could. When we learned enough and were old enough to realize what it was all about— when we felt Christ was in our lives and that we were ready to accept that—then the rest was up to us."

So, when Terry Bradshaw was in the fourth grade in Shreveport, Louisiana, he told his Sunday school teacher he wanted to be "saved." She sat him down and explained what he'd have to do. The following Sunday, when Brother Buck gave the invitation, as the congregation sang the final hymn at the morning worship service, Terry Bradshaw publicly gave his life to Jesus Christ.

Later when Terry was in the seventh grade, he began to doubt his own faith—and that of others he thought of as Christian. As a teen-ager, he saw hypocrisy in the church and sin and lust among his elders.

"I just couldn't handle that," he said. "I never quit believing, but I certainly had lots of questions. I couldn't believe the behavior of some of the people who were running around professing to be such great Christians. Then, when I became a senior in high school, I rededicated myself to Jesus.

"By that time I knew a whole lot more about my own faith and what God could do with a person's life. When we are young, there's so much we don't comprehend about God and about life in general. There's a certain amount of emotionalism involved with being saved, but emotionalism without intellect gets you nowhere. You have to read the Word, study the Bible and grow in faith. If you accept Christ and sit around waiting for your life to change, I just don't think it's going to happen that way. You have to work, pray, and study to bring about change."

At Woodlawn High School in Shreveport, Terry Bradshaw wasn't even the starting quarterback until his senior year. "We lost the state championship 12–9 to Sulphur High because I threw an interception."

Terry described his high school experiences this way: "All I cared about was playing ball. I loved football and track. I held the national high school record in the javelin. My classroom work was second in my life. I had enough natural classroom ability to get by, and that's all that mattered to me. I could have excelled in the classroom had I not been so involved in sports. I was a super Christian and a super jock, but I guess by most standards I'd be called a dull guy."

There were a good many college scholarships waiting for Terry, however, most schools wanted him for track. But he desired to play football "because there was no money in throwing the javelin." He counseled with his high school coach, Lee Hedges, whom Terry describes as "a beautiful man, a dedicated Christian gentleman who I respect more than anyone else in the world outside of my own family."

His decision about college was clouded in controversy and even drew the attention of the National Collegiate Athletic Association. He originally signed with Louisiana State University.

"There was tremendous pressure put on me to go to LSU," he remembered. "Charlie McLendon was the coach and it was every Louisiana kid's dream to play for the Tigers. I'd have been thrilled. But even after signing a tender to go to LSU, I knew I had absolutely no confidence in my ability as a quarterback. I was clumsy and awkward. Whatever skills I had didn't come easily. I can't remember a day in high school or college when I wasn't throwing the football, and a great friend of mine, Tommy Spinks, probably caught more passes from me than everyone else put together.

"It boiled down to this: I wanted to play, and I was afraid that if I went to LSU, I wouldn't get to play."

So Terry switched to Louisiana Tech at Ruston, about seventy miles from home. "When I was a freshman, Tech had no leadership among its seniors. There was no dedication and as a consequence, not much performance on the field. I was so upset that I tried to transfer to Florida State the following summer. I even went down to Florida State that summer to check things out. They were really after me. But suddenly things cooled off. I always had the feeling someone at Tech blew the whistle, so I came back, but very reluctantly, for my sophomore year. I wasn't very optimistic about my college football career at that point."

It was at this time that Tech hired a new coach—Maxie Lambright out of Southern Mississippi. Bradshaw knew his offense—three yards and a cloud of dust. Lambright was as enthusiastic about the forward pass as Darrell Royal and Woody Hayes, who've said that there are three things that can happen when you put a football into the air, and two of those things are bad. Then Tech hired Mickey Slaughter, the former Denver Broncos' quarterback, as coach of the quarterbacks. That was the blessing Terry Bradshaw needed.

"He became like a big brother to me. He knew I was a passer, and he worked my tail off to make me a better quarterback and a much better thrower. He did great things for my confidence and helped me develop poise and courage by assuring me I was good and could do the job. Besides, he was somebody I could lean on."

Despite Slaughter's instruction and encouragement, Bradshaw didn't win the starting job until halfway through his sophomore season.

By the time he was in his junior year, Bradshaw had football fans around the country wondering, "Who's that phenomenal quarterback down at Louisiana Tech?" By his senior year, everybody knew. Meanwhile, his religious life was full. He witnessed in churches all over the South.

The turning point in his collegiate career came in the third game of his junior season.

"I was four-for-sixteen passing in the first half against Memphis State. It was a miserable first half, and I remember sitting in the locker room thinking, 'Well, God, I'm really blowing it. I'm choking and I'm really terrible.' Then I said to myself that I would go out there and show the world in the second half. My whole attitude turned around. Here I was given a beautiful opportunity to excel, and I was wasting the chance and squandering my God-given abilities. So I charged out in the second half and completed nineteen passes in a row. We didn't pull out a victory, but that game turned my entire season—perhaps my career—around totally."

Even after such a brilliant college career Terry Bradshaw didn't allow himself to entertain many thoughts about playing professional football. It was a dream, and a far-fetched one, until he played and starred in the Senior Bowl at Mobile, Alabama. Suddenly, he was the top draft choice in the nation.

The kid from the country was going to the Pittsburgh Steelers. "I was terrified. I didn't know anything about Pittsburgh except what I'd read in textbooks. All I thought about were steel mills and coal mines. When I saw the Steelers on television, I thought they were terrible. I signed my contract and had a fine pre-season as a rookie. But when the bell rang and the games began to count, it was disastrous. I was totally frustrated. I couldn't do anything right. I lost my confidence. For the first time in my life I heard boos. Everyone criticized me. It was all new to me, so I was ready to quit and go to full-time preaching. I just wasn't mature enough to handle any of it.

"One writer called me pro football's number one flop. I became defensive and rude. We're all born with a sinful nature, and at that stage of my life, all my sins came out of me. I thought maybe I wasn't the Christian I had believed I was. When I went home after that terribly long season, I did a ton of thinking, but I resolved to go back and give it one tremendous shot. I did, but for the next three years I was void as a Christian. I wasn't active at all. I didn't take part in Bible study, I had no prayer life, and I didn't give a hoot about anything except football.

"The team stumbled around for a couple of years and so did I. I just separated myself from Jesus Christ. I got married in 1972 to a beautiful and intelligent girl who had been Miss Teen Age America. But it was a mismatch. We had no prayer life, no church life. I let God down, I let her down, I let myself down. We finally got divorced because there just was no other solution. I was devastated by my failure.

"I began drinking and running around and was a failure on the field, too. The fans booed me off the field, and I was benched. Everything was wrong. It didn't get straightened around until October of 1974 when I turned back to God and asked him to help me."

Terry Bradshaw has found a beautifully moving correlation between God and football. It is a simple and uncomplicated thing with no frills, much like the Steelers were when they won the Super Bowl and much like the Green Bay Packers were when they were winning it all every year.

"The secret to football is preparation," he explained. "You have to study your opponent, know his weaknesses, and know where to attack him. You have to know your own strengths and weaknesses and capitalize on them. Our team wasn't fancy. Everyone knew we'd run the ball, and they had to try and stop us. Everyone knew our defense was strong. We were disciplined and well-prepared. It's that way with Christianity.

"I had no game plan and my defenses were down, so I let myself drift away from God. And you can't do that. You can't deviate from his path. We all have that old sinful nature and we're vulnerable to sin and temptations, and that's where Satan works on us. So we have to work hard and prepare and know that God is our quarterback. We have to let him call the shots and have faith that he'll carry us through."

In a recent crusade Dr. Billy Graham said he's likely more tempted than the average fellow "because the Devil would love to get his hands on Billy Graham." Terry Bradshaw has felt those great surges of temptation, and the more success he enjoys, the more frequent the temptation.

"But I know I now have the strength to cope with it," he adds. "Because of the world in which I work, I probably meet a lot of characters I wouldn't ordinarily meet. I meet lots of professional people. Some of them want to use me. There are groupies and hangers-on, but to withstand those pressures you must be strong in your faith and have that daily talk with God. Without him, we're nothing."

Has Terry Bradshaw ever prayed to God for a victory on the

football field? "I could lie and maybe it'd sound better, but I have prayed for victory. God knows what we're thinking so we might as well say something as think it. I've prayed for success, and I've prayed to do well, but I've also done it because the better known I am and the more popular my name is, the more I can use that stature to witness for him. I never take any glory personally. I always give the credit to God.

"During my early years when I was thinking about becoming a full-time minister, I was more or less hoping for a call to the ministry. I even thought maybe I'd had a call and ignored it. But I realize now that this is my calling; not everybody is called to be a preacher. God needs Christians in all walks of life. That's why it's so great to be a professional athlete and a Christian who's very much in love with God because I can be a good witness for him right where I am every day.

"I thank God for Jesus Christ. You know, if I left the game of football today, I'd feel I have been very successful and very fortunate. I wouldn't trade any of the bad times because they've made a man out of me. You can't play forever. Someday I won't be 'Terry Bradshaw, football player.' I'll be Terry Bradshaw, rancher, farmer, or businessman. None of that super star stuff. I'm just happy to be alive and happy to be a Christian and to know that I am saved. God truly has worked miracles in my life. I can always have God."

The turnaround in Terry's life has caused professional changes. He and coach Chuck Noll have what Bradshaw calls a "professional relationship." "I look upon him strictly as a coach, and I'm sure he looks at me just as a player. And that's fine. He's the boss, and he's proven he is a great coach and a talented man. I'll abide by his decisions, no matter what."

And what about the news media? "I used to cry to the press because I wasn't playing or because I got rapped, but no more. I don't read the sports pages, and I don't watch the sports on television. They have a job to do, and so do I. I've been made fun of, ridiculed and portrayed as a dumb country boy. I'm not going to volunteer for an I.Q. test to appease some writer. But I hold no bitter feelings. None at all. The main thing is that I'm able to roll with the times, good or bad."

Bradshaw disdains a showy religious performance with his teammates. "Look, we have forty-three guys in there. They're of different faiths, creeds, and colors. Faith is a very personal thing, and you just don't barge into a crowd grabbing guys and telling them to 'get right with God.' If I started whooping and hollering about Jesus, it'd turn them off faster than anything. I just try to be a good guy. Everyone knows I'm a Christian. If my example helps someone else, if my open witnessing helps lead someone else to Jesus, then that's wonderful and I'm glad."

Some National Football League performers who were asked about taking part in this book declined. Some said they simply didn't want to talk about their faith. Others didn't feel their stories were interesting enough. Of all the athletes contacted, Terry Bradshaw's reasons for participating made the most sense: "I am a Christian and it's a way for me to publicly give my testimony. It's a good way to communicate and to witness for Jesus Christ. Besides, I feel God wants me to do it. I feel better when I witness. Jesus talked about witnessing (Matthew 10:32) 'Whosoever therefore shall confess me before men, him will I confess also before my Father which is in heaven.' He promised that if we witness for him down here, that he'll witness for us in front of God. And he also said if we deny him here, he'll deny us before God the Father.

"It couldn't have been made any plainer than that. Jesus promises that if we tell everyone we love him on earth, that if we are Christian and let him live in us, when that day comes when we can no longer walk the earth in a physical way and stand before God, he'll be our witness up there.

"I want to hear Jesus say 'Father, Terry has been witnessing and promoting you down there, so I'm sticking up for him up here.' I mean, what greater partner could you have on your side?"

What greater partner, indeed!

2

Adam, Eve, Moses, and Then . . .

More than thirty years ago a preacher named John Carrara was making the revival circuit. His was a powerful message. The stories about his own childhood, his family life, and his conversion made strong men tremble. He was an Italian Catholic who converted to Protestantism and told of his transformation in a compelling book called, *Why a Preacher and Not a Priest*.

When John Carrara's parents learned he was attending religious services in a Protestant church and that he was discovering a meaningful spiritual experience through those services, the penalties were severe. The beatings from his father were almost unmerciful. He was excommunicated from the church and alienated from his family.

Folks at the First Baptist Church on the corner of Sixth and Palmer streets in Middleport, Ohio, were dramatically moved by Reverend Carrara's message during an evangelistic crusade. It was Carrara's strong persuasion that led many young people to go forward and publicly confess their sins and turn their lives over to Jesus Christ.

There has been no John Carrara in the life of young Randy Gradishar. There will be no beatings from Frank Gradishar. When the elder Gradishar reads this book, or when someone tells him that his son's testimony is included on these pages, it will be his first knowledge that his son no longer is a Roman Catholic. Randy is not certain what the reaction around the house in Champion, Ohio, will be.

It has nothing at all to do with the respect that he feels for Frank and Ann Gradishar. And he is as certain of their love for him as he is that he loves them. It is simply that Randy Gradishar found Jesus Christ, and thus discovered himself, outside the faith that he took for granted as a child.

When he was a boy growing up in Ohio, Randy thought of

his existence as anything but extraordinary. "Champion is a small place outside of Warren," he said. "While Warren is a good-sized industrial city, Champion has a population of about seven thousand. A lot of the people there own their own businesses. They're pretty independent. We were neither rich nor poor.

"My dad owned the grocery store, the B and J Super Market. I started working there when I was eleven years old, and I did pretty much everything there was to do. I started out as a stock boy and later on got promoted to the butcher shop. It was all right, but in high school I knew it wasn't what I wanted to do for the rest of my life.

"My grandparents were born in Czechoslovakia and Yugoslavia, and until they died, my parents spoke those languages around the house. My dad also owned a nine-hole golf course even though he never played golf. He's always been a hardworking guy, but if I have one regret about my childhood, it's that he was always concentrating so hard on making a living for his family that I never really spent much time with him. We didn't do much of anything together.

"My mother did most of the driving when I had to go here and there to play sports. I was on a swim team when I was in the fifth or sixth grade. Then I played Little League and Pony League baseball, and we had some pretty decent teams. I used to go to the YMCA and Mom used to drive me there. She even drove me on dates when I was a kid.

I went to church regularly, as did my mother—dad just went some of the time. But we didn't talk about it much around the house. I always knew there was a God, but that's about it. I guess it was just something we took for granted."

For a long time, that was all right with Randy. He was so occupied with athletic competition there was little time put aside for anything else.

He drew knowledge and inspiration from his high school football and basketball coaches, Al Carrino and Roger Rogos. It was those coaches who persuaded Randy and convinced some colleges that he was a lot better than your run-of-the-mill high school senior. By the time he was ready to graduate from Champion High School he had scholarship offers in both football and basketball.

"I was really surprised," he said. "Coming from a little school like Champion, I was all-nothing. We played other little schools like Liberty and Newton Falls, and I didn't think anybody noticed us. Then all of a sudden, guys from Ohio State, Penn State, and other schools were coming around to talk with me, my parents, and my coaches. The first scholarship offer I had was from Bowling Green, and I was so flattered I almost made my decision right there."

Randy, who stood more than six-feet-two and weighed some two-hundred-ten pounds as a high school senior, played tight end and linebacker on the Champion High School football team. He was particularly impressed by the visit of Penn State coach Joe Paterno, was put out because Michigan's Bo Schembechler did not pay him a visit (he made a telephone call instead), and was tempted to go to Purdue. Ohio State had been represented by Lou McCullough, an assistant coach. But once Woody Hayes found his way to Champion, Ohio, all the other schools were knocked out of the box.

Randy remembers the day Woody came to call: "We had a day off from school and I was working at my father's store. Someone from school called and said Woody Hayes was looking for me. Before I knew it, he was in our store. He spent most of the time talking with my dad. Naturally my father was very impressed. Dad had been in combat during World War II, and he and Coach Hayes spent most of the time talking about the war. Hayes didn't spend much time talking with me at all, and for a while after he left I was a little put out about it. But the more I thought about it, the more I was impressed by the man.

"He talked about my classroom work and my future after I got out of college. He asked about my two older brothers and how I was getting a greater opportunity. I guess he took it for granted I could play football or he wouldn't have been there in the first place. Coach Hayes really didn't have to concern himself about building me up. I was just thrilled that he visited me and expressed an interest. It was clear that he was honestly interested in me as a person, and after playing at Ohio State for four years, I still feel that way. You know, a lot of coaches give you the same old pitch, but Coach Hayes was different.

"For my father, it was like God walking into that store. My father's a hard worker who believes very strongly in this country, and he's always had great admiration for Coach Hayes. I knew right then I was going to Ohio State."

Spending four years at Ohio State—three seasons on the varsity—did nothing to change Randy Gradishar's opinions of

Woody Hayes. His volatile behavior, his sideline explosions, or his refusal to talk with newsmen after disappointing defeats—Randy understands all these things. He writes it off to a combination of Coach Hayes' intensity and what Gradishar calls the badgering Woody gets from some segments of the press.

"His football record speaks for itself," he said. "He's one of the most knowledgeable people I've ever encountered. As a person, he always had the time to sit down and talk with a player about anything. You could go to Woody with problems about school or your personal life—anything at all. And you just knew he was genuinely interested and concerned, even though you sometimes might not like the answers he'd come up with. Woody Hayes has been like a second father to me."

Not everyone in Champion thought Randy Gradishar would make it big at Ohio State University. One fellow made a fifty-dollar bet that he'd never start a game, never even run down the field on the kickoff team. "But all that did was give me more incentive when I finally got to college."

"There were lots of players at Ohio State who were bigger and stronger. They had been all-Americans, all-staters. I was all-nothing. But I had a lot of desire to succeed. I remember the very first day on the freshman team. We were told to go out and scrimmage against the varsity because the big guys needed some work. Right away, the big fullback, John Brockington, came busting through and stuck his helmet right in my sternum. I went back to the huddle and nearly started to cry. But I learned something. I learned I could take it. And I learned I could play."

Randy played so well he's now considered one of the best linebackers ever to play for Ohio State, and after only two seasons with the Denver Broncos, he is regarded as one of the most talented linebackers in the National Football League. Randy Gradishar won lavish all-America honors with the Buckeyes, and up until the time he joined the Denver Broncos, he had never played on a losing football team.

In 1975, when the Broncos lost more than they won, Randy Gradishar experienced his first losing season. It took some of the fun out of football: "I'm not saying that winning is everything; I don't want to give that impression to anyone. I think I can lose gracefully, but it's a disgrace to lose when you should win. I've tried to play like I always have, but all of us make mistakes in football as well as in every other phase of life. But the Denver club has never developed a winning habit. And I just happen to believe that a team can develop a tradition for winning as well as for losing. We're a young team, and I think what we have to do is work a little harder and believe in ourselves a little more—get on the right track and kick that losing tradition."

When Randy worked at his dad's grocery store, Janet Tricker was working at her parents' Dairy Queen shop just across the street. She'd see to it that he got free milk shakes and once in a while she'd write a note to him on the lid.

"When I got a break from work, I'd run over to the Dairy Queen and sit on the milk cans and she'd bring out milk shakes, hot dogs, and dilly bars. When we started dating, she'd do the driving because she was sixteen and I was just fifteen. I always kid her and tell her I felt obligated to marry her after all the free food she gave me. She's really the only girl I ever had. Janet went to Otterbein College a year while I was finishing high school, and we both dated other people a little bit, but not much. We went together for about seven years before getting married."

When Randy entered Ohio State, Janet transferred there. She was raised in a Methodist atmosphere, but she attended Catholic services on campus with Randy.

"That's when I started doing some thinking about my faith," said Randy. "Janet isn't anti-Catholic or anti-anything, but she made me do some thinking on my own. I had been going through the motions for years. I was just doing what I was expected to do—attending church, confessing my sins—doing my duty. It really had no meaning for me. I began to have lots of questions about God, religion, my own life, and where I was going. I was looking for answers that I wasn't finding in my own church life.

"I'd had no Bible training at all. I didn't know a thing about Christianity, really. The only Bible people I'd ever heard about were Adam and Eve and Moses. But then I started learning about God and his son Jesus Christ. I began reading the Bible, and gradually, I began to find answers that had eluded me before."

Randy and Janet were married in the summer of 1973, just after she had graduated and right before he began his final year at Ohio State. She taught school to help support them that season. They decided on an unusual wedding ceremony.

"My folks naturally wanted us to have a Roman Catholic wedding, but Janet's folks preferred a Methodist ceremony," he said. "So we solved it. We got married at the home of my basketball coach's mother in Newton Falls, Ohio. We had both a minister and a priest. I guess maybe it blew everyone else's mind, but Janet and I liked it."

Rex Kern, a dedicated Christian and former Ohio State quarterback, got Randy involved with some Bible study programs during his senior year at Ohio State. When he went to the Denver Broncos, he was strongly influenced by players Calvin Jones and Tom Graham, who served as chapel leaders for the squad. They asked him to attend the Pro Athletes' Outreach Conference in Dallas in February of 1975. It was that conference that finally caused Randy to turn his life around.

"I went down there looking for answers," he explained. "I wondered why I should accept the Lord. I wondered which faith would be best for me. At that time, naturally, I believed in God, but it wasn't a working faith and I wasn't going anywhere with it.

"At that conference, I saw athletes who were really involved with Jesus Christ. They were happy people and they had something I wanted. I just kept asking questions. There were pro football players who had come through tragic problems with drugs and with their marriages. They had seen everything go sour, yet they had found answers. And I wanted those answers, too. I know God was knocking at my door.

"Doc Eshleman talked with me several times and asked me if I was ready to let Jesus Christ come into my life. I told him I was still searching—I was confused, but he understood. I just wanted to get home and try to straighten things out in my mind. A lot of people had told me it was simple—that I needed only to open up my heart and let Jesus in and that he'd take over.

"John Niland had overcome some problems, and I talked with him. I met John Hannah, Norm Evans, Bill Ferguson, Billy Andrews—all of them were outstanding Christians and my head was spinning. But I needed time to think. I knew my decision had to be intellectual as well as emotional. A couple of months after I got home I accepted Jesus Christ as my personal Lord and Savior. I knew then I could do it and stick with it.

"And now it all makes so much sense. Although I had never read the Bible before, I do now. And the more I read, the more

I understand about life and about myself. It just made good sense to ask the Lord to come into my life and take control. He can do the rest. And now I just read, study, and witness the best way I know how. I'm sure others have had much more dramatic conversions. In my case, I'd always believed in God. It was just that I didn't know him personally.

"Now he's changed my life in a lot of ways. Even in football, I used to be nervous before every game. But this past year, I made it a practice to pray to the Lord and tell him that I was putting all my trust in him—that he was my strength and my shield. I never worried about getting injured, and I knew I could go out and do my very best in every game.

"God gives us our talents. In my case, he gave me some athletic skills. He gave me the ability to perform, and all I have to do—all he really expects of me—is to acknowledge that gift. Some people try to complicate things, but being one of God's people isn't very complex at all."

Asked how he thought his parents would accept the news of his new faith, Randy responded: "I'm not sure. I don't even know if my parents are aware that I've been converted. I was a Roman Catholic for eighteen years and never really accepted the Lord into my life. But I know what I believe, and I am much more concerned about what the Bible has to say, and what Jesus Christ teaches, than I am about doctrine and man-made laws. I'm sure I don't have all the answers. But I am learning day-by-day about the Christian faith. All I can say is that I have accepted the Lord, I know that he is working in my life, and I know he is for real. Also I know I am growing spiritually and am a better human being. I know Christ hears and answers prayer, that he died for the sins of the world, and that he is the only hope for a better world."

As we finished our talk, I remembered the words that a good man scrawled on a piece of paper one day: Wise is the man who gives up what he can never keep to gain what he can never lose.

3

The Faith of a Child

As a child he went to a modest church, heard a simple and uncomplicated message, and did as he was told.

Later, the church became bigger and the message more difficult to understand. It seemed, as someone once wrote, that the preacher was confusing the King's message with the ambassador's fancy.

Church was a ritual, a social event, and little more. Finally, the muscular man became a religious dropout, still believing in God but unable to grasp the full meaning of his faith and not knowing much except that God is.

By the time he entered his third year of professional football, the boy had become a man. Moreover, he had become the finest tight end in all of pro ball. He understood his blocking assignments and his pass patterns but little, really, about his faith.

He walked down the hall of the dormitory at the Cranbrook School toward the training quarters to get taped. The Detroit Lions were to play the Philadelphia Eagles that night. A group was closeted in a small room and a friendly giant of a man was leading the players in the pre-game chapel service. That, too, had become nothing more than a ritual.

If he got up in time during the regular season, he'd sometimes drop by the chapel service held on the morning of the game. If he slept in, that was all right, too. It didn't matter much one way or the other.

Usually, some local personality would share his testimony or an outside speaker would give the message at the chapel service. To our man, though, it was more show than anything else. He felt at the time most of his teammates were there to pray for a good game or pray they wouldn't get hurt. He wasn't deliberately trying to judge them nor to put them down. It was just that not much registered.

The day at Cranbrook was different, though. Charlie Sanders

had allotted himself time for the pre-game meal and his customary ankle taping. He had no plan to attend chapel service. But as he got to the door, he heard the speaker talking about the difference between religion and Christianity.

"I had always thought the two were the same," Charlie recalled. "I had always heard about religion, religion, religion—from the first time I can remember anything at all. I really hadn't heard much about Christianity.

"So I decided to listen. This guy had me interested right away when he said that religion is man's effort to reach God and that Christianity is God's effort to reach man. He said that Christianity is a gift handed to us by God Almighty and that all we have to do is to reach out and take it, give our lives to him, and let him assume control."

The speaker was Ira Lee Eshleman, the self-appointed "chaplain to the pros," whose missionary work among pro football players is one of the most inspirational in the world.

Charlie Sanders always operated under the theory that a religious person was necessarily a Christian. His faith was drilled into him as a youngster; it was the kind he never questioned until his late teens.

Some years ago, Dr. Billy Graham explained the difference between "interest in a religious revival" and "a revival of religious interest." A group of students noted increases in church giving, construction and attendance, and asked Dr. Graham if this signaled a religious revival sweeping the country. Dr. Graham explained that there was more curiosity, more of a revival of religious interest—but he saw no evidence of a genuine religious revival.

"That's pretty much what I was going through in my last year of high school and through college," said Sanders. "I was curious and confused, but I never really lost any of my faith in God. I just didn't know anything about my faith and didn't know how to find anything out until Doc Eshleman came along.

"To me, church had become a nice place where nice people went to hear a nice man tell them how nice they were. I always thought the purpose of church was to provide answers, not ask questions. I don't mind being challenged and being stepped on and made to feel like a sinner, but most preachers I listened to just confused me. They were too fancy. They seemed to be preaching for their own enjoyment, and it was all over my head. I just wasn't getting any message out of church. But when Doc explained the difference between religion and Christianity, he did it in simple layman's terms that a child could understand; we're all children of God and the message of Jesus Christ, while sometimes baffling, really is a simple one. All he's telling us is to take up our cross and follow him. Now, that's not very complicated, is it?

"I had heard people talk about having a personal relationship with Jesus Christ but I was missing that. I just accepted the fact that there is a God and let it go at that.

"But when Doc Eshleman put it on the line and said that all a person had to do was to invite Christ into his life, and truly mean it, wow, it felt like a ton of weight had been lifted from my shoulders. I saw it right away. Here I'd been going to church all my life, from the time I can first remember, and I never really understood the full meaning of life."

Charlie Sanders' early years were spent in Richlands, North Carolina. He can't remember his mother, who died in childbirth when Charlie was two years old. It was understandable that Nathan Sanders would make the church a central part of the lives of his three sons. After all, Grandpa Clarence Sanders was the pastor of the Baptist Church in Richlands.

A half dozen years later, Nathan Sanders remarried, left the farm country of Richlands and moved his family to Greensboro where he became professor of engineering at North Carolina A & T. There they attended a Lutheran church, "because my folks told us to, and we never questioned their judgment."

So Adrian, Charlie, and Nathaniel Sanders attended church like good little boys and accepted it as a fact of life. It was the place to be, and they were there whenever the church doors were opened. But soon there were questions in Charlie's mind. The family had attended a Baptist church in Richlands; why were they going to a Lutheran church in Greensboro? What's the difference? The Baptist church had been warmer, friendlier with a much more open expression from its parishioners. The Lutherans, he felt, were much more reserved, some even stodgy. They were too formal, too organized. The congregation didn't seem to be caught up in the service. There was no outward sign of emotion.

Charlie remembers that at the age of eighteen, when he was entertaining offers to play football at dozens of colleges and universities, he sort of "tuned out" religion and the church.

"I knew there was a God but I didn't know how to reach

him. I didn't have that personal relationship that people talk about. I could look around me, as I do now, and understand that only God could make the universe, make the trees and grass die then come back to life and all those things. But that was all. As a matter of fact, I couldn't wait until I got away from home when I was eighteen because I thought I was a man. I could then make my own decisions. And one of those decisions was that I would go my way and let God go his. I did that until the day I met Doc Eshleman."

Just as Doc Eshleman introduced Charlie to a living God, it was Kenneth Henry who first introduced Charlie to organized sports. "When I came to Greensboro, I met Kenny Henry. He was my age, and he was already into sports. I used to sit and watch him and admire his skills. That's when I decided to go into sports."

Right off, it was apparent that God had given Charlie unique skills. They were to carry him to stardom on the high school level in Greensboro and on to the University of Minnesota where he met his wife Georgianna. Today, the Sanders' family includes four daughters.

On the day Doc Eshleman reached Charlie Sanders with the explanation of religion and Christianity, he couldn't wait to tell his wife. "She's always had a strong faith, and she rejoiced when I told her I was finally beginning to understand mine."

After the chapel service that afternoon at Cranbrook, Charlie sought out the much-traveled evangelist. This whole business of simply inviting Christ into one's life seemed too easy. "But Doc assured me it was just that simple. All I had to do was invite Christ in, and mean it, and then let him take over the controls of my life. When I left that room, I knew there was something I was going to do. I didn't know what it would be, and I didn't know just how I would do it.

"That night I went out and scored three touchdowns. I really felt so light and so free. The following week we were getting ready to play another exhibition game against the Browns in Cleveland, and I couldn't think of anything else except what Doc had said.

"I was in the dugout at Cleveland waiting to be introduced. I just closed my eyes and invited Christ into my life. I remember looking up toward the sky, but all I could see when I opened my eyes was the top of that dugout.

"Then I went out and had a horrible game. It was the first game as a pro when I didn't catch a single pass. After the game

I said to myself 'I wonder if he heard me?' Then I remembered what Doc had said: If you truly mean it, that's all that counts. After the game we had our little group prayer, and I got down on my knees and prayed again. I told God, 'Hey, I'm serious about this.' I thought I'd better make sure he heard me.

"I've had problems of one kind or another like everyone else. I had them before I totally accepted Christ, and I've had them since. But since I've had him on my side, I know there's not a single problem I can't handle.

"But I have to confess this: After I accepted Christ, I began to slip away from him a little bit. I put Charlie Sanders on the throne and God in the background. We all have egos, and I let mine get a little out of hand. I'd do something and say to myself, 'Charlie did this or Charlie did that.' I forgot that I'm number 88 and that God has to be number one.

"I struggled along that way until one night we were playing the Colts in a pre-season game in Tampa. I honestly believe that God slapped me on the behind because that's the night I hurt my shoulder. The first thing that popped into my mind was 'Why me?' Then I knew why. It had been too much 'I' and 'me', and not enough of him. As I was being wheeled into the operating room, I found the answer. I truly believe it was God's way of spanking me and reminding me that he's the top man. He just put me back in my place, that's all. And that night I put him back on the throne for good. I realized then that if a person is going to walk with God, he has to walk all the way, and he has to walk God's way.

"To this day, whenever I make a decent block or catch a pass, I always say 'Thank you, Jesus.' When I walk onto the field, I say thanks to him because I'm just glad to be there and I know I'm there because of the talent he gave me. When the game is over and I walk off the field, I thank him again for having given me the opportunity to play and for taking care of me during the game. I just put myself in his hands and let it go at that. I know he'll take care of me his way, not Charlie's way."

Doc Eshleman didn't learn of Sanders' full conversion until three months afterward. The Detroit Lions had just played the Atlanta Falcons, and it had been a particularly rugged game in the physical sense. Sanders said it was the worst beating he ever took in a football game. He had a scratched retina, a hip pointer, a hyper-extended knee, and got the wind knocked out of him. The trainers practically carried him from the field.

As he lay exhausted on the training table, a solitary figure made his way through the locker room and extended a huge hand to the Lions' star. It was Doc Eshleman.

Joe Schmidt, then coach of the Lions, said "That man needs a doctor, not a preacher."

But Charlie wanted to see Doc, not a doctor.

"I did it," Charlie told Eshleman.

"You sure did," said Doc. "You played a great game."

"Not that, Doc. I mean I did it. I accepted Christ as my personal Savior. I invited him into my life."

Today, Charlie Sanders has found a church that fills his needs. He sees the congregation as ordinary people looking for a simple way to have a relationship with God.

"I still don't understand a whole lot about the Bible," he says. "But the answers are there, even if they sometimes are hard to find. The Bible is difficult to understand in some places, but we often complicate his Word with our own thinking. All I try to get out of it is what God is saying to Charlie Sanders.

"I classify myself as a struggling Christian. I doubt if anyone on earth can call himself a true Christian all the time, because we all sin, every day. I ask forgiveness for my sins, and I ask God to help me be a better Christian each day of my life."

Charlie Sanders keeps his Bible close by, and lately he has been concentrating on Psalms: "The Psalms really relate to the person and show just how much God can do for that individual."

Charlie Sanders sees fewer "doubting Thomases" around the National Football League these days. Time was, not long ago, when witnessing was a scarce item. No more.

"I'm seeing some beautiful things among the younger players especially. Kids are reaching out for something, and many of them find there's something missing in their lives. When they find Jesus, they realize that he was what was missing in their lives. Some years ago, our chapel services weren't very well attended, and we had the same tiny little group every time. Now it's really grown, and I see the same thing happening all around the league.

"Now, I'm not saying the Christian athlete is less physical. He'll go just as hard on every play and try to knock you back on your heels. But he'll be the first one to reach down and pick you up. Then, on the very next play, he'll try to knock you down again. I think the feeling is, 'OK, I'm a Christian, but my physical gifts come from God and I'm in the NFL through his blessings. So I'm going all out for God, because it's through him that I'm here.'

"Sometimes I'm hurt and confused by some of the things that happen in this game. All of us get caught up in the excitement of the moment, and it's a game of action and reaction and sometimes there's just no time to think before you act. It's a game in which you can lose your temper very easily and say and do things that you wouldn't say and do if you had the time to think. It bothers me that I don't have time always to stop and think before I act."

Sanders is still bothered by an incident in a 1974 game against the Oakland Raiders. "We have a Bible study class with some other players each week, and we had just talked on the previous Thursday about the violence of pro football and the difficulty in controlling tempers.

"Then, during the Oakland game, one of the Raiders' players took a really cheap shot at me. I just reacted and jumped up. I didn't swing, but everybody knew that Charlie Sanders did not have love in his heart at that moment. I was disappointed in myself, and I'm sure God was disappointed in me, too.

"I worry about my posture with my teammates in times like that. I still lose my temper, and I don't like that. I have to work very hard to do the Christian thing. But I know I have been blessed with talent, and being caught up in a violent sport is part of that—but it's a test for me as a struggling Christian, and it's the one thing I haven't conquered."

Charlie Sanders knows his football days are limited. He bears the scars of many battles and down the road he'd like to combine his athletic skills with his Christian experience in a youth endeavor.

"My goal is to work with young people. I feel I owe this world a great deal. Somehow I feel I've been placed in the game of football for a special reason. I'd like to have my own camp or youth center and teach young people the wonderful tie-in they can have with sports and Christianity.

"You know, a lot of people believe in Charlie Sanders, and they like him because of what he can do on the football field. Football has been a big part of my life. But it won't mean a thing to me after I'm out of it, and it won't mean a thing to those people who like me now. I'd like to leave the game knowing that I've given people something more important than some passes that I caught or touchdowns that I scored."

4

A Gentle Giant

It was Thanksgiving eve and in sixteen hours the Los Angeles Rams would do battle with the Detroit Lions. The Rams figured to win the game, mainly because of their defensive capacities. The offense during the 1975 campaign had been good enough, but it was the defense that really enabled the Los Angeles team to do so well.

The man who had anchored the defense for so many years was relaxing before the battle. He had seen all the films he needed to see. He and his teammates knew that the Lions were not loaded with quality players. But at the same time they knew the Detroit team could scramble and gamble, and that because it was a traditional holiday game, and that because it would be on national television, and because it would be played in front of the Lions' home fans, the psychological edge would be with the Lions.

Over the years—fourteen of them at that time—Merlin Olsen had learned not to take any team for granted. Too many times he had seen teams lose games they should have won because they had not felt enough respect for the other team. He had seen too many victories snatched away because of inadequate mental preparation. Too often he had seen the thing announcers always refer to as "momentum" turn in the underdog's favor and create touchdowns the heavily favored team could not overcome.

But on this night, Olsen was guarding against that sort of thing. He and his roommate, defensive end Fred Dryer, talked at length about the necessity to stay mentally sharp as well as physically prepared for the upcoming game.

The Rams were both the next afternoon. They whitewashed the Lions 20–0 and clinched a division crown for the third year in a row. It was a victory Olsen and his teammates hoped would lead the Rams on toward the Super Bowl.

As much as he cared about the game that has earned him

a handsome living and reputation, Olsen has always maintained a strict posture about the importance of football. To him, it remains a game. It is to be played, and once over, it is to be left on the field. Although he enjoys the game, its fellowship, discipline, dedication, and rewards, it still is a game—and not a way of life. It is a means to an end, rather than an end in itself.

One of the things that bugs big Merlin Olsen about our society is the praise and adulation placed upon sports stars. "So many parents take a ridiculous attitude toward athletes," he said, "that they actually press images that sometimes may be faulty upon their own children. They say to young children, 'I want you to be like Super Jock' or they say, 'I hope my son grows up to be like so-and-so.' In nearly every case, all they really know about the athlete is what's been on television or in the newspapers and magazines. The guy could be a bad human being for all they know, but because he gets an enormous amount of publicity, because he's making good money, and because he has certain physical skills they think that's enough of an example for their own kids. The whole thing is ridiculous."

It was pointed out that this has been a problem for years. Even when Eisenhower and MacArthur were the big war heroes, more children of that era still wanted to be like the current sports stars, and parents of that era pressed the images of sports celebrities on their children more than other types of heroes.

"I know," said Olsen, "and that is one of the frightening things about our society. Maybe the time has come for us to begin to think realistically about the heroes we'd like our children to have. Much of what we become, I think, can be traced back to our early dreams. It's the old philosophy about a man being what he thinks he is. Within certain limitations, naturally, I believe most people generally develop the kind of personality they want. It makes me wonder how smart we are as parents if we continue to fall into this trap."

When Merlin Olsen was a boy growing up around Logan, Utah, he most wanted to be like his father, Lynn. The senior Olsen was a soil scientist for the Bureau of Reclamation. He spent much of his time developing water projects for rural areas that lacked water.

As a boy, Merlin thought his mother never slept. The demands of nine children kept her busy all the time.

"Sometimes I'd stay up past midnight," he recalled, "and Mom would still be up washing or ironing or doing some other chores.

And it wasn't uncommon for me to be up at 5:30 in the morning—and she'd be up, hurrying around getting things done. She was always bright and cheerful. I guess I thought she just went without sleep."

The Olsen home wasn't very large, to begin with. First there was an older sister, then Merlin, and then seven more children followed. The house was expanded to five bedrooms. Merlin recalls bunk beds, a coal burning stove; northern Utah winters sent the temperature dipping to twenty below.

"For a long time there wasn't any heat in my room, so we'd come in and dress by the stove," he remembers. "If nothing else, it got you out of bed in a hurry on cold mornings."

Both Olsen parents came from strong pioneer stock, and that, plus a Christian upbringing, produced a household full of love and hard work. Merlin remembers rugged times but no deprivations:

"Sure, I occasionally wondered what life would be like if I were an only child and we lived in a big house on a hill. But I was fortunate to have good parents, and I always knew they loved me. Even though they were busy with the job of survival, I wouldn't trade my family life for anything in the world. I'm glad we had to battle and scramble to get things done. It wasn't easy, still I always had the feeling that whatever we needed we could get, and I always realized that there was absolutely nothing my folks wouldn't do to see that the kids were taken care of.

"There was always enough to eat and clothes to wear. Even though my parents worked tremendously hard, all of us kids today still have great memories of family fun. We did things together; more people should do that today—I mean, make it an absolute rule. We always took our leisure as a family. We spent a lot of time fishing and hunting, and in nice weather every Sunday after church we would take a picnic up to the mountains. Those are very special memories for me."

Not long ago, one of Merlin's acquaintances expressed some conflict about a decision—whether to use his tickets to one of the Rams' home games or go to the beach with his children.

Merlin's advice—and it was strong advice, too—was to, by all means, spend the day with his family at the beach. Football games come and go, but when children are gone—well, Olsen didn't think the decision required much thought at all.

Because of his early family ties, Merlin is determined to make time for his own three children, and he is dedicated to the belief that today's attitudes toward marriage and family life are eroding that kind of good life.

"I want my kids to be better than I am," he insisted. "I'd like them to be smarter, more honest, better in their relationships with people. Kids always need to feel they are wanted and loved. I had that. I want my kids to have it. Kids need that kind of security. I'm sure we all are products of what we have seen and felt, especially in our early years. I would hope that I can be as good a parent as my folks were to me."

Over the years, football fans have come to know Merlin Olsen pretty much as the hulking number 74 who sacks National Football League quarterbacks and devastates opposing runners. In recent seasons they have seen him in a new dimension—without helmet and uniform—in public service announcements played frequently on national television during NFL telecasts. He is as he appears to be—large, friendly, articulate, sincere.

"I think people have to care," he explained, "and I believe you can almost divide the population between people who care and others who don't. I don't think we always listen to that voice inside of us that says, 'Hey, some folks are hurting and you have an obligation to help them.' But I think we all feel, to varying degrees, some pangs as the result of the way we have been brought up or the kind of experiences we have had in our lives.

"I have a special soft spot for kids, and not just because I have three of my own. I'm very close to them, of course, but I also enjoy talking to youth groups and church or YMCA groups. Kids deserve some time."

For more than twenty football seasons Merlin Olsen has performed under pressure—the pressure to win. Possibly the pressure is greatest in the professional ranks where one's pay, not a monogram or letter, is at stake.

"Ultimately, though," Olsen said, "the most significant pressure is the pressure we place on ourselves. That is, if we're any kind of human being at all. We all feel it. Either you choose to accept the pressure and do something about it or you shrink from it. If you want to be a success in football or anything else, you have to turn the knob."

Despite overwhelming success in professional football, Merlin Olsen has remained pretty much a low-profile guy. Even though he is a friendly giant, he is not a demonstrative one. To him, his religion is a very meaningful but at the same time a very private thing. He is not a man who is easy to categorize, nor does he want to be. This is not to say he is difficult to understand. Quite the opposite is true. It is just that whatever good he does—and the amount is significant—he chooses to do it quietly and without fanfare.

Does Merlin Olsen hear a different drummer? "That's a tough question," he said. "It's commonplace now for people to use the expression 'doing my thing,' but we all look for a place to be comfortable. I haven't totally found my place yet. I've enjoyed much of what I have seen and been a part of. I have very few complaints about my life. One of the things we're all concerned about, if we do any thinking at all, is security, and in finding rock bottom answers.

"I'm not as involved a person as I should be. You see, I was raised in a very devout Mormon home. My parents have done missionary work. They've paid their own expenses to coordinate agricultural programs for the Indians in New Mexico, Arizona, and Oklahoma, helping them to learn more about agriculture.

"It is not a religious mission if you're talking about religion in the usual sense, but there surely is something very Christian about dedicating yourself to helping others. That kind of religious tradition is very much a part of me."

Merlin makes no secret of the fact that professional football being a Sunday game has taken him away from some of the participation in his church—nor any secret of the fact that this has bothered him more than a little bit.

Merlin Olsen is a learned man with deep feelings and a great sense of responsibility. Asked what he finds in his faith that sustains him, this was his reply: "There is great peace of mind and tranquility among Mormons. I'm not saying we have all the answers and other folks have none. What I'm saying is that my faith works for me and my family.

"Mormons are generally happy people. And they will take care of themselves and others. We have wonderful youth programs that stress not only religion, but recreation, and an opportunity to get involved in music and drama."

Merlin is greatly concerned about the image being presented to the young people of this country. "Take a look at your average television news show," he suggested. "If it lasts thirty minutes, we are often treated to twenty-seven minutes of crime and violence and you have to ask yourself how young people can concentrate on things that are good and wholesome when it would appear that the world is one big rotten apple.

"It worries me that these things are considered so important. Our young people are soaking all of this up, yet somehow we expect them not only to be bright and clean but understanding and full of faith in tomorrow. What are we giving them to build on? What kind of foundation are we providing for them?

"We've put tremendous burdens on the young people today. So much knowledge is available and things are happening so quickly in today's society—I'll tell you, it amazes me how well they do cope with what's happening. The thing that frightens me most are the seeds we've planted and the directions we've taken as adults. Take our natural resources, for example. We've raped this country, and instead of tapering off, we're accelerating. We're fortunate to have the abundant resources we do have. And we still have a beautiful land, and if we change some things now, we can keep it that way for our children and other generations on down the line.

"Kids today have an awareness that their parents didn't have, and awareness comes first. We have to have awareness before we can do anything. We've done a few things but only because we were forced to do them. For example, when the price of oil shot up we started looking for solutions. I guess we only learn through pain. But if we're not careful, in the very near future we'll be suffering great pain from neglecting the warnings we're getting now."

The natural question for Merlin Olsen, then, was about the violence that permeates the world of professional football. Because violence is so commonplace in the pro game, it has rubbed off onto all levels of play, even at the little league level.

"Violence is built into the game of football," he explained. "There's no question about it—football is a violent game, a rough game. But it is important that we remember it is still a game. If it were played by people bent on doing violence, then it'd be a terrible thing. Fortunately, that is not the case.

"The thing that has always been important to me—and I'm sure to most other players—is that you don't have to hate people and you don't have to want to hurt people to be a good football player. It's just not within my nature to force myself to hate people or to try to hurt someone. I get cheap shots sometimes, and I have had people go out of their way to try and hurt me.

"I've been chopped a few times in my career, but I can't think of a single guy in the league right now I would want to deliberately injure. Maybe on a particular afternoon some guy has hammered on me or grabbed my face mask a few times, and I'll look for the chance to pop him back. But that's what I call a sturdy reminder. We have our own code in pro football, and it's not to be violated. If you violate the code, you leave yourself open for that kind of retaliation."

Crowd behavior all across the land is a major problem. Fans are not only more vocal, but more violent. Throwing snowballs, even golfballs, out of the stands at players has become commonplace. Stadium repair bills are skyrocketing because of the destructive nature of today's fans. Violence in hockey has become a major problem, and some basketball coaches are asking for police escorts to and from the court because of unruly spectators.

"I'm concerned about that sort of thing, and I'm confident other players are too," said Merlin. "It indicates to me there's lack of respect everywhere. In Green Bay the fans killed Dan Devine's dog because they didn't like his coaching. They did some other things that just stagger your imagination. He's not the first coach to be abused, and he won't be the last. What this tells me is that some people simply have lost their perspective. It's ridiculous. Football must be a game. For some people it has become something it was never intended to be. No one is more serious about the game than the athletes, but at least we can leave the game on the field, for the most part.

"But there are so many good and wholesome things that come out of football. It may sound corny, but the important, positive things are still there, and so are the great lessons to be gained from football. A person can learn fantastic things about the spirit of teamwork and cooperation, dedication and sacrifice, the value of hard work, and the rewards that come to those who are willing to pay the price.

"Those who are willing to make the great sacrifices and who are determined to do a good job ultimately are rewarded for their effort and work. And it's the same way in the world outside of sports. Maybe the rewards don't come so quickly and perhaps not so many people notice because there's not so much ballyhoo. But I think the kinds of things we do on the football field are reflected in the things that happen in the real world. Football players live in their own little cubicles, and we somehow condense life into one-week segments: We die one Sunday, we are born again on Monday, and we really come alive the next Sunday. And we do it over and over and over again. The difference is, if we die more than a few times during the course of the season, there's no Super Bowl!"

In the beginning, Merlin Olsen was more than willing to talk, to be courteous and friendly and hospitable. It is not his nature to be anything else. But he wanted to keep his religious beliefs and his inner thoughts about such things as morality, family life, home, and God to himself. It is just his nature to want to maintain a posture of privacy about the things he holds most dear. But in thirty years of interviewing athletes of every size and description in every field of sports combat I have never interviewed anyone more humane or more articulate than the friendly giant of the Los Angeles Rams.

5

A Missionary in Pads

The year 1967 had not been what you would call a banner season for the good-looking young man from Colorado.

He hyper-extended his knee while in rookie camp. That's a bad enough injury for anyone, but it's especially telling on a kicker. Even when training camp began in mid-summer, the injury had not healed, and he was kicking poorly. Finally, he asked the club for two weeks off so the knee would have a chance to heal.

Two weeks later he pronounced himself ready to kick. The club gave him two choices—Canada, or Akron in the bush leagues. He chose Akron because it was close to Cleveland.

Then the Akron team folded and he headed back to Cleveland. There was a car wreck, and he wrenched his back, twisted his pelvis, and wound up with a kicking leg a half inch longer than his left. He spent the rest of the season in pain and getting splinters in his back side from sitting on the bench.

"I was a failure and a disgrace," said Don Cockroft. "The whole season was just a wipe-out. I knew I was a failure. The Cleveland Browns knew I was a failure and the fans knew it. I was ready to quit football."

Don Cockroft had accepted Jesus Christ as a boy of thirteen. He had been listening to Pastor Eugene Verbeck at the Trinity Church of the Nazarene in Fountain, Colorado, just outside Colorado Springs.

"I was sitting in the balcony with three of my buddies," he recalled. "We were just goofing around when the pastor came to the close of the service and he said some things that really hit home. We all stopped chattering and started listening. Then he gave the invitation. I felt led to go and pray, and perhaps to invite Christ into my life. But there was no way I was going up there by myself, and I made up my mind that if one of the other guys went, then I'd go, too. Sure enough, one of them went.

So I went to the altar and invited Christ into my life. I said, 'I believe; I don't understand all of it, but Lord, it says if we invite you into our lives and depend on faith, you'll come into our lives and our hearts and live within us.' And that's just what I did."

When he was offered a two-year contract to kick the football for the Cleveland Browns, Don Cockroft had no lofty thoughts about his abilities. But he had decided that if he made it, he'd use pro football as a platform for his belief in Jesus Christ. That first-year-failure brought about an exhaustive search for the real meaning of his faith.

"I kept asking myself *why,* and I couldn't come up with any satisfactory answer," Cockroft told me. "I went back home to Colorado after that first miserable year and continued to search and wonder about my life and its meaning. One day in church, I felt God was asking me to give up pro football. I felt he was saying to me, 'Don, if you really want to know what I have planned for you, you'll have to put all these other things out of your life.' I was thinking perhaps I'd be asked to go to Africa to do missionary work."

Don Cockroft refused. He said he knew his life as a Christian wasn't what it should be. He was morally sound and tried to do all the good and right things. His life was up and down, but there were too many downs and not enough ups. He was not growing, not maturing, as a believer.

"In essence," he recalls, "I was saying that football was my god. I had promised to use it as a platform and to use it to glorify God and here I was unwilling to give it up. I know now it was the greatest mistake I ever made."

He likened it to the story of the rich young man who asked Jesus Christ what he had to do to inherit eternal life. Jesus told him about the commandments, and the rich man assured Jesus he knew all about them and had kept them since childhood. Then he asked Jesus what else he should do—so Christ told him to sell everything and follow him. The rich young man was not willing to go quite that far.

During that winter Don got his physical problems corrected, but he continued to struggle with the spiritual ones. He worked out each day in Colorado and by the time the Cleveland Browns assembled for training camp prior to the 1968 campaign, he was eager, confident, and kicking the football extremely well. The kicker competing for the job, Errol Mann, was sent to another team. Lou Groza, who for years had handled the Cleveland kicking chores, retired. The job belonged to Cockroft, and he responded by leading the National Football League in field goal kicking.

"It was a good season spiritually, too," he remembers. "We had some good Christian fellowship on the team with players like Bill Glass and Monte Clark. Even though I felt I was growing as a Christian, I still knew something was missing. There was an emptiness and it kept eating away at me all the way through the 1971 season."

The 1971 season had not been good by Cockroft's standards. Early in the season he had missed seven of eight field goal attempts, and it was difficult to catch up and produce a good percentage. During the season he reached a decision to attend a Nazarene Bible College session in Colorado Springs in the off-season.

"I was just on a roller coaster," said Cockroft, "and I thought maybe by taking some classes and studying a few courses I might get things straightened around. Then in February of 1972 I got the same kind of message and command from God that I had heard four years before. I was in the very same church, and an evangelist named Dr. T. W. Willingham was in the pulpit. He didn't pull any punches at all. He was a real firebrand, a super speaker. There are two worship services in our church, and as he spoke during the first service, I was really moved. Normally I'd have gone to my Sunday school class after the first service, but this day I knew I had to stay and hear him again and get some things straight in my mind. The Lord was really speaking to me.

"I told my wife Dianna I felt I had to stay, so she agreed to wait for me. After the first service there was the customary invitation to pray. I knew what I had to do. At that point I was finally bent to God's will. I was ready to tell him, 'OK, you take over and run things. I'll give you all I have.' If it meant giving up football, I was ready to do that. I had to have within me the willingness to sacrifice what I thought was my career. After a lot of thought, prayer, and soul-searching, I was ready to do all those things."

A favorite passage of Scripture that Don came to rely on so heavily in those days was, "Trust in the Lord with all thine heart; and lean not unto thine own understanding. In all thy ways acknowledge him, and he shall direct thy paths" (Prov. 3:5-6).

In other words, on that cool morning in beautiful Colorado, Don Cockroft was not attaching any conditions to his relationship with God. There was no option clause, no loopholes.

"He promised us that if we just trust in him, he'd take control of everything," said Don. "At that point I simply said, 'Take over.' I didn't know what way he'd have me go, nor what he'd ask me to do. But right at that time of my life, I knew that whatever he wanted, I'd do it willingly. I began to study his Word more than ever, because I was searching for answers. I figured that through studying the Bible God would show me what he wanted me to do, and how he wanted me to serve him. Then, I came across a verse that has stuck with me ever since— in First Corinthians where it says God is not the author of confusion but of peace.

"It occurred to me then that perhaps God didn't want me to go halfway around the world to testify for him and that maybe he wasn't asking me to witness full-time in a pulpit. But perhaps he wanted me to witness for him right where I was, in professional football, in my everyday life. All he really wanted was my life, and my willingness to put him first, to let him be the coach and general manager of my life. There were no bolts of lightning or anything like that. It was just a quiet deal with God, and after the second service that day I went to the altar as a witness to publicly profess my faith and trust in him."

When it came time to prepare for the following football season, Don Cockroft went about his physical matters in much the same way, except with perhaps a bit more intensity. Saved at thirteen, Don felt that he finally had become sanctified—by his own description—set apart for the Lord's service.

"It was a new slate," he said. "It was a new beginning. I enjoyed football, and it gave my family a good living, but I wasn't really worried about the possibility of giving it up. I knew I might have to, but it didn't overwhelm me. And I've been fortunate in having only one woman in my life, and Dianna is a wonderful Christian woman who has understood all these doubts and fears. You know, shortly after I made my full commitment in 1972, she told me she had turned her life over totally to God, too. Dianna has a beautiful testimony as to how she has been blessed by God."

When Don came to the Browns' camp after the turnaround in his life, the Cleveland club had drafted another kicker, George

Hunt of the University of Tennessee. The competition for the kicking job was intense, but Cockroft won the job—even though Hunt was kept around on the taxi squad. Cockroft had one of his finest seasons and when people ask him if he knows why, he answers:

"Lots of people will say it was the competition, and good competition does help to bring out the best in people. It's true that George was pushing me all season, and our new special teams coach, Al Tabour, helped me. But I feel my success came because I put my life into God's hands. And I worked hard, knowing deep inside me that everything would be all right, no matter what.

"I never want to miss a field goal or an extra point, but once I turned my life completely over to God I got rid of that terrible fear of missing. I still worry about it, but not like I did before."

Working hard has been an integral part of his life. Being brought up on a farm with four brothers meant lots of hard work. Up at four in the morning, out in the barns or fields working two or three hours, coming in for breakfast, going back to work, coming back in for a mid-day meal, sleeping for an hour, then going back out for more work—that was the Cockroft childhood. And there was a tremendous togetherness in the home.

"We did everything together," he recalled. "The thing I remember most about my childhood is that we had daily Bible devotions right after breakfast. We had a short Bible lesson each day, and very early in life I began to see there was something real to the faith my parents had."

Just as his parents gave him early understanding of God's Word, so today Don Cockroft is able to help others to that same understanding.

"I'm not a trained minister," he said, "and I don't preach. All I do is share my testimony and my faith through the Word of God. It's great to know that the Lord does come, does intervene, and does speak to people. It's amazing what he can do with our lives if we just let him inside us.

"As for me, I pray that he someday will use me in full-time Christian service. I have seen wonderful progress throughout football. So many more young players are coming into the game with a knowledge of Jesus Christ so I know there is great work being done in the colleges and high schools. So Christ is moving among the young people. You see a lot more Bibles in football camp than ever before. And many more athletes want to get involved in chapel services, prayer, and Bible study groups.

"Some of the most involved people I know, admit that they used to laugh behind our backs when we went to chapel service, but they came to realize that we had something they lacked. They now know that the Christian athlete has an inner peace and contentment because he knows God lives in him, and that because God lives, he can have life eternal.

"You know, in the Gospel of Luke there is that beautiful story about Jesus feeding the multitudes and instructing his disciples on what they should do with their lives. And he makes it very plain that we must deny ourselves, take up our crosses daily, and follow him. He's telling us to stay close to him, and whatever trouble we might have, if we stay with him, deny ourselves, and really lose our lives in him, we'll be all right.

"I know that's what God said to me and that's what he is saying to everyone. Following him is the name of the game. Even though we need him and cannot have eternal life without him, he needs us, too, to show other people what he has done for us."

It would not be fair, nor totally accurate, to conclude the chapter about Don Cockroft's faith without including a personal note about our interview. It had been a tiring drive from Michigan to Kent, Ohio, where the Browns were in training. There were unsolved problems back in Michigan and he could see that the interviewer was moved by his testimony and his sincerity.

As the other players hurried down the dormitory hall, headed for the practice field, Don Cockroft spent additional minutes in prayer with another human being—all because to him the game of football is not nearly so meaningful as the Game of Life.

6

From Rituals to Realism

Joe DeLamielleure is a Christian. And it's okay if his family and friends cannot quite comprehend what is happening. Joe and his wife Gerri have had some difficulty sorting it out, too. While they have been in love with each other for almost as long as they can remember, they have been in love with Jesus Christ only a few years.

When he was attending school at St. Clement in Centerline, Michigan, Joe DeLamielleure began and ended each day with a prayer. Once he got to Michigan State University, he slept in when he should have been at Mass, and said his prayers only when he had something definite in mind.

"Growing up with twelve years of Catholic education," said Joe, "I was very much aware of God, but that was the extent of it. I can't say as I had much of a personal relationship with God."

University life was, in one sense, disillusioning for young Joe DeLamielleure. He explained it this way: "There were only twenty-three players on my high school football team and when I got to Michigan State as a freshman, it seemed like there were a thousand guys around. I got a scholarship, and I guess I thought I should be right up there starting, but they had other players listed in front of me.

"Right away I had second thoughts about it. I figured maybe I should have gone to a smaller school. My high school coach had warned me about getting lost in the shuffle. All that seemed to matter was football. But all your confidence is taken away your first year. It was drummed into me that staying eligible was the big thing, and taking easier courses was the way to do it. I didn't worry too much about my grades. I got right into the program with everyone else, lifting weights, football classes, learning the plays to get ready for my sophomore year."

Once in college, Joe pretty much ignored the rituals of his faith except just before the football games.

"There was no one at State to tell me to get up and go to church or go to confession," he said, "so for three years I didn't go to mass on Sunday. I wasn't living at home. I was my own boss. And right away, I got lost as far as my faith goes. But right before the games, I'd start being real good. Maybe it was superstition, I don't know. Maybe I figured the Lord would help me out if I were good. Maybe it was part of my mental preparation for the games. I didn't feel I was being a big hypocrite because I wasn't all that bad.

"I'd go to mass before every game. Father Lammert was our chaplain. He's a super Christian and he knows what it's all about. But the things that being a Christian are really about—I never gave those a thought. I never really had any fellowship with Jesus Christ. I just took things for granted."

All through college Joe had received inspirational letters from an older brother, Darrel. Joe came from a family of ten children, Gerri from a family of eight, so family ties are meaningful.

"Darrel kept encouraging me to read the Bible," said Joe. "I thought he was a good guy and he meant right, but I actually didn't pay much attention. Darrel and one of my sisters, Marlene, left the Catholic Church and found what they'd been missing in their lives."

Joe DeLamielleure got his degree in criminal justice before leaving Michigan State, but by that time it was obvious his career was in professional football. He had a great deal of conversation with pro teams and their scouts, and he had been assured he'd go high in the draft.

"I used to watch these guys on television and dream about playing football with them," Joe confided. "I remember saying to myself I'd be happy if I got a scholarship to go to college. When I got it, I felt I'd be happy if I made all-Big Ten honors. Then it was all-America. Then it was being drafted, and I wanted to make the all-pro team by my third year. So now, I've made that, and I don't know if I have any goals left. Money isn't a big thing with me—it's just a means to an end. Sure, I want to be paid for what I do, but I can't get all that fired up about it."

Joe DeLamielleure nearly saw his professional football career go down the drain before it got started.

"Gerri was working, and she was in the early months of her pregnancy," Joe recalls. "I had played in the Senior Bowl and got twelve hundred dollars for that. In all, we had a grand total of fourteen hundred dollars. So I told her to quit work. I was pretty sure of getting some decent money out of the pro draft. All along, I was thinking how happy I'd be to have $5,000, but when the Buffalo Bills picked me as a number one choice, all of a sudden I started thinking maybe I'd get $50,000! I guess I thought we had it made, and I forgot all about God's part in my life. I guess he had served his purpose again—after all, he got me drafted in the first round, just like he got me the scholarship and all those other goodies.

"It must have been March, and our savings had dwindled down to about two-hundred bucks, and I told Gerri we'd better go on up to Buffalo and sign that contract."

There was just one simple procedure before the signing. All draftees had to take a medical examination. Joe flunked his. Something about a heart defect.

"My whole life was shattered," he explained. "I had no money, a pregnant wife, no job, nothing. All the things I had wanted were destroyed. On the way back to Detroit from Buffalo, Gerri and I sort of came to the realization that perhaps God was trying to teach me a lesson. After all, we had each other, and we had him."

The next few weeks were tortuous. Joe imagined he had terrific heart pains. He thought about dying. Then, he thought about living. After all, he had never had any real heart pains. He had no shortness of breath. He had played football for years with no apparent problem. Perhaps the doctors in Buffalo had been wrong. He decided to go through the heart tests at the world-famous Cleveland Clinic. Doctors there decided it would be all right for him to play football. Buffalo doctors, in turn, sent those tests to Atlanta where it was confirmed by other experts that Joe would not endanger his health by playing. So it was back to Buffalo to sign a contract and to look for a place to live.

Joe DeLamielleure quickly won a spot on the Buffalo Bills' offensive line—the group O. J. Simpson has praised so highly for opening the holes for him. Among the first players who warmed up to him were Robert James and Ted Koy.

"I learned quickly from them what it meant to be a Christian," he said. "I went to the chapel services and at first I felt a little strange. Then I began to talk openly with Doc Eshleman about my faith, what it could do for me, and what it could mean to me. All of a sudden, things started to become clearer for me. There was no bolt of lightning nor anything like that, but I came to the understanding that the Lord, for some reason, gave me the talents to be a football player.

"He didn't give me the talent to be an outstanding public speaker—but Jesus doesn't ask that of everyone. He asks that we be witnesses. And that's what I am doing. I've learned that I can't use Jesus like a prescription and just call on him when I need something. I have to let myself be used by Jesus Christ in whatever way he sees fit to use me. I still get off the track—I guess everyone does—but I have a strength now I've never felt before. I've learned that being a Christian is a life-style.

"My first year with the Bills I started attending Bible study groups and the following season I went to the pro football conference. Those activities have really helped me grow as a Christian."

The only problem the DeLamielleures face now is one of labeling, and for them it is no problem. For members of their families, it might be ticklish. Said Joe: "All I know for sure is that the Lord is guiding me through my life, and Gerri and I are like newborn Christians. We're really having an honest-to-goodness fellowship with Jesus Christ and we're getting something out of our faith. We really don't discuss the change in our Christian life with anyone except my brother Darrel and my sister Marlene.

"You know, I went back to Detroit for a wedding and there must have been thirty guys there who had the same dream I had—that they could make it in pro football. And I was the only one who realized those hopes and dreams. But now my dreams and aspirations have changed. Sure, I'm grateful for what I have and for the chance to play football. I got my scholarship. I made all-Big Ten, and I made all-American, and I got drafted and got to play in the National Football League.

"But more importantly, I found a better person down deep inside of myself. I've found a more fulfilling and enriching life. I've learned that it's not enough to say prayers then go around taking God for granted. You have to be involved with him. For a long time I was just aware of the presence of God. Now I understand more fully that God sent his son Jesus Christ to die on the cross for my sins. All I have to do is give thanks and witness for him. And that's what I'm trying to do."

7

The Deacon's Son

It's a good thing Harold Jackson's daddy forced him to go to Sunday school, church, prayer meetings, and all that. The way Harold sees it now, he needs all the help he can get each Sunday afternoon.

After all, he's only a shade heavier than 170 pounds—a bit frail by professional football standards—and he takes a fearsome beating week after week as the top wide receiver for the Los Angeles Rams.

"When I was a kid my folks made me become involved in the church," said Harold. "I guess when I got to be a teen-ager, I was like everyone else. I resented having to do anything, and I wanted to find out what it would be like not to have to go to church and take part in all the activities. When my folks finally let me make up my own mind, it was only a week or so before I was back in the thick of things. My whole life had been church-oriented, and there was just no way I could make the break."

It is true, then, that the apple does not fall far from the tree. And it is true that if you raise up a child in the way that he should go, he will not depart from it.

"All I wanted to do was play ball," said Harold. "I don't think kids ever want to be forced to do anything, especially these days. But religion was such a major part of our life that there was no way to avoid it. I mean, our lives were centered around the church. There was a deep involvement and a meaningful commitment. But when I tried to break away, I found that I was involved and committed, too. I wasn't just doing something out of habit. I needed God then and I need him now. I feel that when I go out there on a football field—and it's not just because I'm smaller than a lot of the people I play against—I believe I need someone on my side. And the One I want on my side is Jesus Christ."

Eartha and Ollie Jackson introduced their son Harold to this kind of life in a little Baptist church in Hattiesburg, Mississippi. In those days, being black in Hattiesburg wasn't the best bargain you could strike. Harold remembers that life, for his family, was a "struggle." But he abhors the use of the term "poor."

"It was just that we didn't have much," he said, "but I don't think we thought of ourselves as being poor. There were other folks who had it a lot more difficult than we did. But my folks never let things get them completely down. As tough as things were, my father always tithed. It was a sacrifice to be sure, but he believed that a person should make a definite sacrifice for the Lord and you'd be blessed for it."

Just as Ollie Jackson put a goodly portion of his wages from the Mississippi Power Company aside for church tithing, so his son Harold contributes generously to the same church.

The Jacksons learned early the true meaning of the term "sacrifice." There were six children around the table and Harold said the Jacksons had everything they really needed—provided they didn't need a whole lot—if not all they wanted.

Years ago, Harry Emerson Fosdick complained that too often we tend to sentimentalize Jesus Christ in poetry and painting and song—when in fact the Savior was a very strong person. Harold Jackson, number 29 of the Los Angeles Rams, has this picture of Christ in his mind:

"He was a guy who went into the streets to deliver something strong, you know. He had to be a very tough guy to do what he did. He had to be pretty impressive and imposing to get all those people to follow him. I mean, he went to a lot of distant places to tell his story and it was a new story, a different story. It wasn't something people could hear just anywhere. And he wasn't selling anything—instead, he was giving it away. Still, a lot of people were reluctant to accept him and he had a tough job. But he got the job done. He knew what he had to do, and he went out and did it, and he did it against some tough opposition. So I picture him as a very, very strong person."

As for his own faith, Harold isn't as strong as he'd like to be. It bothers him that he wavers sometimes, that his faith has not matured as much as he would like.

"I know I don't give God the attention he deserves. I believe, but I could be a lot better. I guess everyone could. But I have to answer for myself. No one can do that for me. And down the road, no one can take my place in the grave. I know Jesus died for my sins, but all of us have to die sometime. And when I think about that I think to myself 'Man, you have to really get yourself together.' I really want to go to heaven, and no one can prepare me for that except me, and I have to do that by following His teachings."

All of us have to prepare ourselves for a better world while living in one filled with anxiety and trouble. The world of the National Football League is sometimes a violent one and for a good-looking bachelor who's also a star, the temptations must be staggering.

Jackson doesn't let the violence of the game get to him. Somehow he manages to turn the other cheek when he's rapped hard with a cheap shot. He explains it this way:

"People have different talents and they play the game differently. I try to keep it clean. I just go out there and do my very best and try to accept whatever comes. I know I have God looking out for me, and I thank him for my ability. I get cheap shots every game, but I try not to think about them. I do my job and go on about my business. I think in the long run, I'll come out ahead. Trying to retaliate by fighting is silly to me. If I can, I like to retaliate by making a good play against the guy who's trying to hurt me."

Jackson has learned that players try to use intimidation—"but it's effective only if a man can be intimidated, and on the football field, I don't think I'm intimidated."

Most athletes do not consider themselves "Jesus Freaks." They consider neither themselves nor those outside the Christian life freaky in any sense. But in recent years there is greater candor and much more openness and willingness to talk about a belief in Jesus Christ.

For Harold Jackson, talking about his faith in God is an obligation. He, and many, many other pro football players read their Bibles in the locker room and on the team plane.

"You know, it seemed for a long time that every time I picked up a Bible I'd find my way to the 100th Psalm," Jackson said. "Now I read it all the time, and it becomes more and more beautiful with every reading.

"It really says it all, when you think about it. We are told to make a joyful noise unto the Lord, to serve him with gladness, to come before him with singing. He made us and we belong to him and we're supposed to be thankful and praise him and be thankful to him and bless him. He is good, his mercy lasts forever and his truth endures through all generations. I love that passage so much I never get tired of reading it.

"I don't think we should be ashamed to talk about Christ. I suppose there are still some people who think a Christian is square, but they just don't understand what's happening, that's all. I've always been a believer; I don't think I'm square, and I don't think people who know Harold Jackson think of him as being square. I'm really not concerned about doing what other people may do. I consider that the most important thing is to be myself. I don't use other people as a guide for my life. Instead, I do what I think is right for me. And believing in Christ is right for me."

All of us have heard the old line about the church walls crumbling if so-and-so walked into the sanctuary. Harold believes the walls of the New Ebenezer Baptist Church in Hattiesburg, Mississippi, would come tumbling down if he did not attend during the off-season. And in the community, Jackson knows he is regarded as a hero, the hometown boy who hit it big in the National Football League. He feels he has handled his success well:

"I don't let the headlines and the attention get to me. I just don't, that's all. I realize I have attained some success, but it's just there. Lots of athletes over the years have let success go to their heads, then they wind up losing what they have. I never go around bragging about what I can do. I just go out there and do what I can and let my performance speak for me. I've had some good games and I've had some bad ones; I try to let it go at that."

Harold Jackson does not have all the things he wants. He's tired of being considered one of the game's most eligible bachelors, and he wants to get married and raise a family. It's not a matter of settling down because Jackson does not consider himself a playboy in any sense.

"I love kids," he explains. "When I'm back home I spend a lot of time with my nephews and nieces. They're great. But I want kids of my own. I love to be around them and work with them. I even sponsor a baseball team back home because I like the kids so much.

"It's very important to select the right mate. And I know the world of pro football is not really conducive to that. It's a pretty fast track, and you meet lots of people who really don't want to know you as a person. I mean, they might be pretty shallow themselves and they're not too interested in finding out what makes you tick. If a guy's not careful, he could meet someone who could really destroy him. The way things are in our society today, it's tough enough to keep a marriage alive—so picking the right partner is super important."

We shook hands. Harold Jackson had made his joyful noise unto the Lord. And now he would go out onto the football field and make it a long afternoon for some defensive back trying to cover him. Then he would pause and thank God for this immense talent.

8

A Good-Time Christian

It has long been a popular assumption that a Christian leads a life of deprivation, that his is an existence of sacrifice, that he gives up fun and frolic when he decides to accept Jesus Christ as his personal Savior.

It doesn't matter to the non-believer that we have been promised that if we lose our lives for his sake, we then shall find our lives. An agnostic once told me that faith in God is a totally negative thing: "Look at your Ten Commandments," he challenged, "they're full of thou shalt nots."

Roger Staubach, the quarterback of the Dallas Cowboys, has for years been challenged by non-believers and kidded about his faith in God. Once, some of his Cowboy teammates gave him a cartoon depicting a man sitting at a restaurant table with his family, while another man was having his fellowship with several bosomy blondes. The champagne was flowing freely. The "good-time Charlie" said to his friends, "Look what that guy over there is missing if there isn't a God."

Roger Staubach feels he hasn't missed a single good thing, except for those things God has in store for him down the road. "I'm not a prude and all through my life I've been a practical joker with what I consider to be a good sense of humor," he said. "But I haven't sacrificed anything. Instead, I have found a wonderfully happy life through Jesus Christ. He's the One who made all the sacrifices for us, so we really don't have to make any. All we have to do is to follow him, believe in him, and put our lives in his hands.

"As for the guy with the girls in the cartoon, he's already saying his life has been sacrificed. He is the one living a miserable life, not the man with his family. A good family life is a vital part of God's plan for mankind. God has given us guidelines to live by. The guy with three girls really is an unhappy and shallow person with no real peace of mind. He's in a real mess.

The family man knows in his heart that Christianity is not a have-not sort of thing. You *gain* blessings rather than give up things.

"My whole life is fun, and I don't feel I'm being deprived of anything at all. Family life is really enjoyable, and a man who follows the dictates of God Almighty has it all together. He has peace of mind. He enjoys sex—it just happens to be with the same girl—his wife."

Roger's strong feelings about family are no accident. As a boy growing up in Silverton, Ohio, a suburb of Cincinnati, Roger had enriching experiences. Some time ago he wrote about them:

"My religious convictions started with my parents. Many parents lecture children on religious thoughts and philosophy, but if a child doesn't see these things practiced by his parents, he realizes the hypocrisy of the whole thing. And the parents actually do him a disservice. My parents were excellent examples of Christianity. They didn't bring me up in the overly religious, fire-and-brimstone-type atmosphere, but rather with a solid foundation that enabled me to determine for myself which direction I wanted to go."

Simply put, being a good and moral person was a way of life, early on. By his own description, Roger was an enthusiastic and active youngster with an ornery streak and a bent for mischief.

Roger was a prankster during Mass and once deliberately gave one of his young friends the wrong cue for ringing the bell. He admits the hero aspect of athletic competition appealed to him when he scored seventeen touchdowns in an eighth grade league. When he went on to Purcell High School, he excelled not only in football, but in baseball and basketball. He was so good that forty colleges and universities quickly began bidding for his talents.

Staubach visited several universities. Some eliminated themselves early because they tried to dazzle him with examples of the fun life of a jock. He was tempted by Ohio State, went so far as to sign a tender with Purdue, knew right off he did not want to go to a school in his home town, and was intrigued by the Naval Academy. Rick Forzano was then an assistant coach at Navy, and he later was to become head coach of the Detroit Lions (and of course later to see his teams demolished by Staubach) and he and the young Purcell High School quarterback struck up an immediate friendship. It was Forzano who brought Roger to Annapolis for a visit and who later suggested that

Roger spend a year at New Mexico Military Institute when his score on the English tests at Navy weren't quite up to snuff.

The one season at New Mexico Military Institute was an overwhelming success, on the field and in the classroom.

Almost as quickly as he arrived at the Naval Academy for Plebe Summer, he met Navy Chaplain Father Joseph Ryan. The friendship that began that summer is one not only of endurance but dedication. When the Dallas Cowboys came to Michigan to play the Detroit Lions in the first game in the Lions' new stadium in the fall of 1975, Father Ryan managed to get time off to come and see the game. And it was Father Ryan who celebrated Mass in Roger's room just a few hours before kickoff.

"He's been like a father to me since my parents died," Roger explained. "I spent a great deal of time with him at the Academy and we grew very close. He's been with me through my most difficult times."

It was Father Ryan who rushed to be with the Staubach family when Roger's mother was in the last days of her struggle against cancer, and it was Father Ryan who delivered the eulogy at graveside.

"Being a Catholic, I figured I'd meet the Catholic chaplain at the Academy," said Staubach. "But I was doubly fortunate in finding a chaplain who not only was a great Christian, but a tremendous sports fan as well. Father Ryan played football in college, loves to play golf, and enjoys competition. He was in Vietnam when I was there, and when I went back to the Pensacola Naval Air Station for my duty, he was there, too. He's always been a source of great strength to me."

Roger's college career at Navy was nothing short of spectacular. He won the starting quarterback's job three games into his sophomore year. As a junior, he led the Middies to the number two ranking in the nation and a berth in the Cotton Bowl against Texas. Individually, he won the Heisman Trophy as the nation's top athlete, was everybody's all-American and cover boy.

The letdown came in his senior year. The Midshipmen were hit by a couple of bugaboos—injuries and complacency. They won only three games and lost to Army for the first time in six seasons. At the end of the season the Navy fired Coach Wayne Hardin, the man who had rebuilt the Middies' sagging football fortunes. Still, the individual honors piled up for the young quarterback from Ohio. He was named the Academy's outstanding athlete for the third year in a row, and to his surprise his

jersey was retired. Said Admiral Charles Minter, Jr., superintendent of the Academy, at the awards presentation: "Such a young
man comes along only once in a great while in the life of an institution. A superb athlete and a complete gentleman, his performance, both on and off the field, reflects great credit on the
institution he represents and on college athletics in general."

There were all-star games later on and Staubach drew great
attention from pro football scouts, even though they knew he was
obligated to spend the next four years with the United States
Navy. He also made another decision to ask his childhood sweetheart, Marianne Hoobler, to be his wife.

"I'm very fortunate in having Marianne as my wife," he
boasted. "She has all the qualities I always wanted in a wife and
mother. When my own mother was dying, Marianne was just
incredible. She took so much of the burden on herself and never
once complained. And she always managed to smile in order to
make things easier for me. And all the while she had our own
children to think about. You know, when I count my blessings—
I count my family first of all.

"Our young people today are so troubled and in a way, it's
little wonder. They hear so much about morality, ideals, and
Christianity, and then see so little of those things. They hear
about concepts from parents and friends and teachers and they
are told to practice things they know are not being practiced by
their elders—in some cases the very parents and teachers who
are handing out the instructions. And they're immediately turned
off. And you can't blame them. Hypocrisy is what they see, and
they turn away.

"This is a very tough thing for the young people. You know,
you find your real relationship with Christ—you have to look
past the human being and look to Christ. But example is important, and I'm very lucky to have had parents who taught well,
and who themselves performed the same way. If today's parents
lived the example they preached, they'd find themselves getting
through to their children more. And their faith would, in turn,
be strengthened just as they're giving strength to their children.

"A person who lives a meaningful Christian life gets additional
strength from the Holy Spirit. If you live the good life, you can
call on the Holy Spirit for additional help and you'll get it. When
I was growing up, my parents talked about religion. Now, they
were not very demonstrative about their faith, but it was strong,
and they lived it every day. In other words, they lived what they

talked. And when they died, they could accept death courageously. My mother knew for months and months she was dying, yet her faith was the kind nothing could shake. She never complained. She knew her salvation was the next thing in line for her. I had those examples with me for years and they'll always be with me."

In the world of professional football, Roger Staubach finds he is not always the Christian he wants to be.

"I'm always going through phases," he elaborated. "Things like jealousy, getting angry, envy, talking about your fellow man—these are great sins. Where morality is concerned, I have no problems. I love my wife deeply, and I am faithful to her. A lot of things have changed over the years, but being faithful to one's wife is something that never, ever changes.

"When I was young, I was taught that it was a mortal sin to french kiss. Today, if that's all kids do, parents everywhere would proclaim their goodness with banners in front of their homes. You know, there have been tons of changes in the Roman Catholic Church and there will be more, I'm certain. As far as I'm concerned, all the changes have been positive ones. I've loved some of the stands the Catholic Church has taken—the one on abortion, for example, I'm very proud of that—and in the area of racial prejudice.

"The celebration of the Mass has changed, but the essentials are there. Just spending the time in church, in prayer, is important. It's hard living in today's world and we need to surround ourselves with all the good things we can. I'm not one who believes we must always have good around us—you know, Jesus Christ walked among some pretty shabby and sinful folks. But you have to keep your eye on God and keep your heart clean.

"I've heard very few priests talk about our responsibilities as Catholics. Rather, today, they talk about our responsibilities as Christians. I think that's healthy. Years ago it was regarded as wrong to even go to a non-Catholic church, but not so long ago I spoke at the biggest Baptist church in Dallas. Gradually the little differences in religions are being broken down. All of us have to become more Christ-oriented and not be so concerned about our own little corners of the world."

Roger Staubach could be out speaking in a church every day of his life—but he turns most of them down because his family is his prime consideration. It is his feeling that Marianne and their four children deserve a great deal of his attention and time—and that by seeing to the major responsibilities of a good, strong family life centered around God he is fulfilling his major Christian function.

He does not strut his faith and adopt a holier-than-thou posture. His own description of himself is that he is a human being with human failings and frailties, but one whose life is Christ-centered.

"God is not a crutch, though," Roger is quick to add. "He is very real to me and every day he gives me peace of mind—that's the main thing—the knowledge that he died on the cross for me. You know, people love to gamble and if they get two-to-one odds they think they have a good thing going. The non-believer is gambling his life span, which is very short in God's eyes, against eternal life and happiness. So many people today are demanding quick answers and quick solutions to their problems and they want the evidence right there in front of them.

"In God, we have to have faith. I've gone through the New Testament and marked the times faith is mentioned. And we are told repeatedly that we must have faith in him, and in his wisdom and in his judgment. I know I've had countless numbers of occasions where I was convinced in my own mind I had the right answer. I mean, I was so honed in there was just no other solution. But others have come along and showed me I was wrong—that there was another solution, and a better one.

"Christianity is like that and we have to really explore God's Word to find his will. All of us have a void, a lack of understanding, because our minds have not been opened up. But I am persuaded that if we follow Christ, someday he will show us the way for all things and give us all the answers we need. That's really what being a Christian is all about—believing in him, and having faith that he will take care of us in his own way in his own time.

"Growing up as a Catholic, I never really studied the Bible. We had Gospels and Scriptures and certain passages from the Bible. But since I have read it, I have found understanding and peace of mind and an enlightenment that I never enjoyed before."

Everyone in the National Football League has known for years the kind of human being Roger Staubach is. Yet he does not try to pound his beliefs into either his teammates or his peers around the league. His is a more subtle approach, witnessing constantly, living the good life, working diligently through the Fellowship of Christian Athletes. He has turned off some fundamentalists because he does not describe himself as a "born-again Christian."

The issue first cropped up during one of Roger's public testimonies in a Protestant church, and a sixteen-year-old girl asked him when he had been reborn. Although he has read of it in the Word, Staubach says he felt no such experience, and that's the way he explained it to the young lady who asked the question. She, in turn, told him he could not be saved had he not been born again.

"I'm just not into the fundamentalist thing," is Roger's explanation. "I grew up as a Roman Catholic and I accepted Jesus Christ as my Lord and my Savior. I have believed in him and his salvation as long as I can remember. This young lady cited a specific time and place for her conversion, but it just didn't happen that way with me.

"There's really no point in arguing with a fellow Christian. I've done it but I'll never do it again. It's just not healthy. I don't believe in putting down another human being simply because his particular faith doesn't exactly coincide with mine. I don't believe in one person judging another. The one thing I can't abide is prejudice, and churches down through the years have been guilty of hypocrisy because of their treatment of people of another creed, faith, or color. Christ teaches tolerance and love of fellow man and makes many specific points about it—remember when he challenged people about saying they love God while hating their fellow man?"

Again, this sort of feeling goes back to Roger Staubach's childhood when his late mother chastised so-called Christians for the resentment they openly expressed about some black families moving into their community. She called them hypocrites for their prejudice. It made a lasting impression on her son.

He is encouraged that today's Christian is much more willing to stand up and be counted on the great issues.

"I see a much stronger Christian in sports now," he said. "Maybe it's the times. Our society has become so permissive in every way and we've seen so much immorality in high places. The reluctance of some of our so-called good people to prevent that, or attempt to turn things around, or to live lives of Christian example, surely has turned some young people away. No wonder they're dismayed and upset. You can't blame them when they see celebrities getting on television talk shows and trying to justify pornography, prostitution, and all sorts of evil things. Our young people have seen an almost anything-goes kind of life-style and we've made heroes out of eccentrics.

"There's so much temptation for them. I know I'm aware of it. I'm in a business where a celebrity or a personality is looked up to and I'm sure I'm tempted more than the average working guy. But every time I go to Mass I pray for the Holy Spirit to strengthen my life so that I can overcome these temptations. There's so much lust and greed today and the question facing all of us is 'How much is enough?' I mean, when do we stop seeking more?

"When I first came into pro football I was told that I never should do anything except for money and I took money the first year. Now, I don't accept money from church-related affairs unless there is a budget for the speaker—and then I insist the money be given to a charity, like the Fellowship of Christian Athletes. I just don't think it is the Christian way to expect praise and adoration for occasionally doing a little bit of good. We have to do things for the glory of God, not for ourselves."

Staubach's coach, Tom Landry, long has been a vital, moving force in the Fellowship of Christian Athletes. There are those critics who have said that Staubach got the edge in the long-standing duel with Craig Morton for the number one quarterback job because his life-style was more palatable to the coach. Roger admits that that criticism has bothered him:

"It's so ridiculous, but it has bugged me over the years. Actually, Craig called the type of organized, planned style of attack that Coach Landry has always liked. My style actually goes against his grain. But no one who knows anything at all about Coach Landry could accuse him of playing favorites. Before the 1975 season he traded away three or four guys who are really super Christian. His football decisions are based on football and nothing else.

"I can't really say that I know Coach Landry all that well. I respect him, but I really don't know him in a personal way. He lives a very solid life. I've heard him speak to various groups, and he's warm and persuasive. But the man just doesn't show his emotions very much on the outside."

Some of Coach Landry's critics have called him dispassionate, cold, even plastic. Says Roger:

"I've seen him throw a clipboard on the sidelines, but in general it's just not his nature to be very demonstrative. In the locker room after a victory he doesn't go around slapping guys on the back. I think he has so much going on in his mind all the time that it's unbelievable. He is a genius, there's no doubt about that. He gets us prepared and motivated to play football."

Roger Staubach resists suggestions that with his background in education, the military, competitive athletics, and his Christian concern, that he'd be an ideal candidate for the political arena. He shrugs it off, citing his determination to turn away from anything that robs him of time with Marianne and the four children. Instead, he likely will turn to coaching once his playing days are over.

"I keep finding plateaus in life," he concluded. "Right now I'm concerned with playing and doing well in football. I love challenges and I'm sure there'll be another one after I can't play the game any longer. I like to work with young people, so perhaps I'll coach.

"Young people, especially today, need lots of guidance and understanding. There is tremendous peer pressure on them. That pressure can make them say 'yes' when they know in their hearts the right answer is 'no'. Young people today live in a world full of disruptions and they have to learn how to cope with them. When kids see the bad examples older people are setting, they have to look beyond that sort of thing and turn to Jesus Christ.

"There are a lot of positive people and a lot of positive things around. The only way to really make it, though, is to drop to your knees and call on Jesus, because he's our only salvation. If young people will but turn to Jesus, he'll come into their lives and give them the understanding, maturity, and confidence to handle even the most difficult circumstances that may surround them. If you're a Christian, you can do anything, and most importantly, you can live forever."

9

A Brand-New God

When he was a student at Bakersfield High School in California, Jeff Siemon took a look around him and saw the world's idea of success. Largely, it boiled down to one ingredient—achievement. That was the measuring stick people seemed to use, so it naturally followed that a bright young man who wanted to get ahead in the world would follow that pattern.

Jeff seemed to be naturally suited for that kind of challenge. He described the pattern his life followed then: "I simply set out to achieve everything I could in those areas I considered to be important. So I did well in athletics, in academics, in student government, in my social life. As a matter of fact, I achieved far beyond even those goals I had set for myself."

Throughout high school, Jeff dated one girl exclusively and the two of them developed a very close relationship. This girl called herself a Christian and often talked candidly about her personal relationship with Christ. One day she asked Jeff what he was going to do with his life. What direction will it take? What does it mean to you? Is there a real purpose to your life? Is there an ultimate goal?

It was the first time anyone had asked him such a tough series of questions. He elected to ignore the questions, but he could never quite get them out of his mind. In many ways, life was full and good, yet inside he couldn't escape the reality of his emptiness.

The issues continued to haunt Siemon as he embarked on what he had every reason to believe would continue to be a successful career—athletically, academically, socially—at Stanford University.

Then came a series of setbacks—the first Jeff had encountered. A knee injury threatened the football career that meant so very much. His social life was not as enriching as it had been. Scholastically, things were tougher than they had ever been.

"I had created a plastic world for myself," Jeff recalls, "and I discovered it was caving in on me. Up until that time, I hadn't really had a confrontation with myself about the true meaning of life. I began to ask myself the questions that had been haunting me. Then I got a letter from Linda. All she wanted was for me to enjoy the peace and the purpose that she was experiencing in her life. The very next day a young man came to our room to see my roommate. The visitor was a member of a campus Christian organization, and he hit on the very issues I had been struggling with. Before he left the room, I made it a point to talk with him. He told me that Jesus Christ came to give man abundant life, a life that didn't depend on circumstance, but a life that could give a man peace even if he were not achieving things he considered to be important.

"The way he told it was that a man considered to be average by the world's standards could have contentment in his soul if he'd just let Jesus into his life. I waited until he left the room, and there, by myself, I invited Christ into my life. Right up until that minute, I guess football had been my god. And all I had to show for it was despair. Suddenly I had purpose and direction. My life really counted for something from that minute on."

Jeff's commitment to Jesus Christ began during his freshman year. It wasn't until two years later that the Stanford University football squad commenced chapel services. There were only five players on hand for the first service.

"We did a lot of praying about it," he said, "and it just kept growing. We asked the Lord to open the hearts of our teammates and to speak to them about the chapel services. By the end of that season we had twenty-five players attending regularly. So we then started a Bible study group that met during the week. It just seemed to multiply, and several players gave their lives to Christ at that time. We had a unity on the team that I'm certain was obvious to everyone.

"Jim Stump, a great Christian gentleman, was working as the West Coast director for Athletes in Action, and he worked closely with us and got us started in the right direction. Those first couple of years were probably the most important in my spiritual growth, because I started from a knowledge level of zero. But through attending several conferences, seminars, and Bible study groups, I was able to make up for a lot of lost years."

Jeff had trouble controlling his Christian enthusiasm in those early years. He'd return from group sessions all fired up and ready to save the world. He found hearts and doors closed.

"I was on such an emotional high I just wanted to share my faith with anybody and everybody, and at times I got severely rebuked. I guess I assumed everyone else would be as excited as I was, and it was most difficult for me to accept the fact that some people weren't very excited about Jesus at all. I tried to argue people into the kingdom of God and I found out later that sort of thing just isn't possible. Only the Lord prepares a heart, and if he hasn't prepared the heart, then you can't get through to people.

"It was a time of great challenge but a time of gradual maturity for me. I know I lacked the spiritual background and when people would refuse to allow Jesus into their lives, it would dishearten me. I know I didn't handle that very well. My pride was hurt because I didn't have the answers. I thought I just hadn't learned enough. People were always asking how I could prove the existence of Jesus Christ, the Savior of mankind. Well, how can anyone prove that? Eventually it becomes a matter of faith. And since I was inexperienced, I often found myself a disappointed young man. But now, through studying God's Word, I know what he said about situations like this. He has a great deal to say not only about Christians, but what to expect from non-believers as well. So now I see things through more mature eyes. I still have challenges, but I handle them better, because of the enlightenment I have from his Word."

It was during Jeff's junior year at Stanford that he met the girl who later was to become his wife. It was almost one of those love-at-first-sight experiences. Said Jeff: "The first time I saw her, I was dating another girl in her dormitory and I happened to meet Dawn in the hall. I was immediately attracted to her genuine warmth and kindness. A little later on I saw her at a fraternity party. I was really captivated by her gorgeous smile. Then a friend of mine mentioned he had seen her playing tennis. I kept thinking about Dawn and her smile, so I finally asked her out. And we've been together since then."

Jeff, Dawn, and their two children now make their home in Minnesota during the off season. They don't like the idea of moving the children in and out of two different school systems. Coping with the demands of professional sports is no problem for Dawn Siemon.

"She's like me in that we both like to be home," said Jeff. "She understands the pressures of professional football and she knows it's my job. And that job involves being away from my family some of the time, but when you think about it, it's not that bad. We have two or three trips during the exhibition season and seven road trips during the regular season. Training camp is the worst time of all, but I can still see her a couple of times a week even then. Actually, though, my work in pro ball really takes up only about six months out of the year."

But Siemon's schedule is busy twelve months out of the year. There are constant requests for speeches and appearances.

"There's more than enough to do to fill my time," he added, "and sometimes I wish I could put more hours in the day. But the Apostle Paul had a much busier schedule than I do, and he said the busier he got, the more time he needed to spend in prayer. I've found that's true with me as well. But I consider my football career a ministry of sorts. There are millions of people in our country today who are captivated by professional football. Athletes have a tremendous opportunity to use their influence in any way they desire. That is why I believe my career in football is a natural and powerful way to share the Good News of Christ with millions. Many read and hear what I stand for and if they are interested in me as a player, they can't help but eventually be confronted with Christ."

Jeff is not sure that being a Christian automatically gives him a position of leadership on the Minnesota Vikings' football team: "I've known lots of fine football leaders who are not Christians, but are well respected as fine team leaders. I merely ask the Lord for presence of mind. Let's face it, football puts one in a spirited, intense atmosphere and it's understandable that some players have difficulty under pressure. I know the Lord has helped me to be rational in tight spots. He's given me the ability to think. That, really, is my testimony on the field. But that's a gift he gives to lots of people, Christian and non-Christian alike.

"But the dimension God adds to me is the ability to accept defeat graciously. Don't get me wrong, I love to win and I play to win. The desire to excel is as great in my mind as with anyone. I've heard it said that you can't be a winner if you lose graciously. I don't think that's true at all. I love to win, but I'm no longer devastated when we lose. I have undergone some of my greatest personal character building after losses."

Football players are heroes, for the most part. We make them larger-than-life figures.

"We all love praise," says Jeff. "That's just basically a human trait. If I said I have never been affected by all the attention we get, I wouldn't be truthful. It's a natural temptation to glory in one's personal achievement, and it's a problem that none of us are completely free from.

"As a linebacker I don't have the problem with attention that some players in other positions do because they naturally get more headlines, and more people are aware of them than many defensive players. But I believe the important thing to realize, when you have a certain amount of talent, in sports or in any other field, is that your talent comes from God.

"If I'm good at what I do, I certainly will have more impact on others. Now, if I were to keep all the glory to myself and bask in it, and not give the Lord the credit, it'd be a different story. But there's no future in that. Whatever personal glory I have goes down with me when I die physically. But the glory that is God's lasts forever. My glory is fleeting, but his will endure for all time."

Jeff feels no particular full-time calling at the moment. He plans to attend Bethel Seminary during the off-season. Down the road, he may consider teaching or coaching at the high school level.

"A prudent man has to think about his future," he explained. "Right now, though, I don't have any leading. I'm certain that the Lord will direct me and show me how I can best serve him. All I have to do is be ready to serve when he calls. And I will be."

10

An Exercise in Faith

It was a foggy Friday night in Hempstead out on Long Island and the interview was winding down. I asked Winston Hill of the New York Jets why he was so eager to take part in this book.

"All I can say is that Jesus Christ died on the cross for all of us," he responded. "That was his gift, his sacrifice for me. I don't think it's asking too much for me to tell my story about my love for him."

It seems that Winston Hill had little chance to be anything but good. When Winston was growing up, his father, Garfield, was minister of the church and principal of the school. He was also, and is, his son's only hero in life.

"It's a great atmosphere," said Winston, "but temptation is everywhere. You can always find ways to sin, even without looking. The trick is to get God in your life, then you can handle all that temptation."

It was then that the Jets' veteran rattled off one of his favorite quotations—one that he believes has strengthened him: "There hath no temptation taken you but such as is common to man: But God is faithful, who will not suffer you to be tempted above that ye are able; but will with the temptation also make a way to escape, that ye may be able to bear it (1 Cor. 10:13)."

As a boy growing up in Joaquin, Texas, a sawmill town of five-hundred near the Louisiana line, Winston's idea of being bad was knocking over a trash can. There were no problems with drugs and none of the permissiveness that permeates today's society. Garfield Hill did not need to be a strict disciplinarian. He got good results by precept and example. He was a reserved and conservative man who wasted few words. When he talked, folks listened.

Winston remembers doing things together as a family and making ice cream. He remembers that there was no running water at the school house, but that the Hill family's needs were met and even though they were poor by today's standards, they may have had a few more comforts than their neighbors.

He was always as big as his peers, but clumsier—"not one of the better basketball players when I was a young boy." His father had been quite an athlete, and Winston loved to compete, to take part. There had been several good athletes on both his mother's and father's side of the family.

"He encouraged me, always," said Winston of his father. "But he never pushed me like Little League parents do today. He just wanted me to try. He kept telling me I was good, but he never told me how good he was. I found out from other people that he was truly a remarkable athlete. He gave me a lot of confidence, and I remember wanting to please him. But I never have felt as though I was competing against any other human being, even since I've been in the pros."

Garfield Hill was not the kind of man who made all the decisions for his wife and three children. Winston remembers the first major decision he had to make for himself. The question was whether to play football.

When he was eleven years old, his father accepted a better job in the school system at Gladewater, Texas. Life changed radically. There were five thousand people in Gladewater and the streets were paved and lighted. It was in Gladewater that the other boys challenged Winston, and it was there he had to stand up for himself "as any self-respecting Texan would do."

He was first introduced to football as a seventh grader, but that year he just watched. As an eighth grader he was faced with the decision on football.

"My mother didn't want me to play but I wanted to because all my friends were playing," he recalled. "My dad said it would be my decision. So I decided to try out."

The very first day, Winston Hill—still bigger, and fatter, than most of his contemporaries in Gladewater, Texas—put his pads on backwards. He was scared to play, and scared not to. It was his first encounter with peer pressure.

"We were thrown in there against the older guys," he remembers, "and I got run over a whole lot. So I just quit. It had been my decision to play and it was my decision to quit. I decided to go on home. I knew my father wouldn't be there right then, so I decided to tell mother and let her soften the blow for him when he came home."

Another decision was made before the Reverend Mr. Hill got

home. This one was made by Mrs. Hill, and with precious little elaboration she marched Winston back to the practice field. Her explanation was simple: You set out to accomplish something, and even though I didn't want you to play, you will not quit before you accomplish what you set out to do. It was your decision to play football. You can quit after you make the team, and not until then.

"It was really embarrassing," he says. "We got back to the field just as practice was ending and the guys coming off the field saw me there with my mother and they knew what had happened. She had a little talk with Coach Curtis Cooksey and that was it. I went back, and never quit."

Winston Hill sees the same pattern over and over again in his life. As a youth, he watched football as a seventh grader, began playing the following year, sat on the bench as a ninth grader, played a little bit as a sophomore, thought he was pretty fair as a junior, and knew he was good as a senior. In college at Texas Southern, Winston followed precisely the same pattern.

Once he got into the professional ranks there was the same parallel. He was cut by two teams the first year, barely made it the second, suffered a broken leg his third, and never missed a game in his fourth season.

His faith in God has run pretty much in the same direction.

"I spent a long time trying to find myself," he explained. "I was always in church as a youngster, but in reality I was a lost person. I believed, but I didn't know much about what I believed in. From the time I was in high school I had leadership roles in church, but I never really did anything that was creative. I just went with the tide and didn't grow as a Christian.

"It seems I was always worried about being accepted. Everyone needs something to be proud of, but I wasn't really doing much. I sang in the choir and was assistant superintendent of Sunday school, but I still didn't do anything with my God-given creative skills. Then I began to learn things about God, and I began to learn much more about myself.

"It's like exercising, you know. You don't reach down and pick up more weight than you can lift. You start with twenty pounds, and after a while that's so simple you move up to forty, then eighty, then a hundred and right on down the line. And it just becomes automatic. It's that way with God. The more one studies and learns and lives by the Word, the more one grows in maturity and strength in Christ Jesus. Now, I don't worry about acceptance. I have a positive identification of myself. I like the person I am today."

Winston Hill never got around to discussing his problems with his father. The fact that he was not fulfilled as a Christian was something he kept to himself.

"I had never tasted beer until I went away to college," he said. "I was really naïve. After that, I felt bad every time I went around my father. I just wasn't myself. I was afraid my speech wouldn't be up to par and I'd slip and say something that would embarrass my parents. I remember when I was home on a weekend my conscience would really be bothering me. I woke my father up in the middle of the night and said 'Dad, we just have to talk.'

"But he took over and wouldn't let me talk. He realized what was going on. He knew what I was trying to say, but he wouldn't let me say it. He just put his hand on my shoulder and said 'Son, you're off in college now and you're going to experience a lot of things you've never been exposed to. But you're a good kid, and always remember that we love you, and more importantly, that God loves you.' And that was the end of it.

"He told me about an incident that happened when he was in college and it appeared he had done something wrong. But he told me things worked out for him, and that they'd work out the same way for me."

Even while he was performing so well in his final season at college, Winston never gave much thought to professional football. But he was drafted in the tenth round by the Baltimore Colts and went to camp. He lasted one week.

"I thought I had a good week," he remembered. "We had an intrasquad game and I beat this other rookie all over the place. He even came up to me after the game and told me he knew he'd get cut but he was just as certain I would make the team. I was really happy. It was a nice compliment coming from another player. Then Jim Parker and Lenny Moore told me I looked good." The then coach of the Colts, Don Shula, gave Winston the jarring news a couple of days later as they met each other going into breakfast.

Aggressive, yes. A prospect, yes. But there was no room for him on the team, and the squad was so large Shula wouldn't have another chance to look at him. No time to look at inexperienced rookies.

Hill was downcast but not dejected. After all, he had been

told by the Denver Broncos of the American Football League that if he got cut by the Colts, they'd like to hear from him. So he called. The Broncos refused to talk with him.

Later, the New York Jets gave him another opportunity. But after a brief time in camp, Weeb Ewbank gave Winston the same speech Shula had given him earlier. You're aggressive and a nice fellow, but we can't use you. He managed to stick around as a member of the taxi squad. By this time, he wanted so desperately to make it in the professional ranks he offered this deal to the Jets: Let me continue to work out with the club and try to learn, and I'll pay my own expenses. The Jets refused, but kept him around at their expense. Not long after that, Ewbank called him into his office once more and Winston felt this would be the ultimate goodbye meeting. But the news was good: The Jets had decided to release another player and give Winston a chance to play regularly. He hasn't given up the job yet.

But as his professional life was rounding into shape, his personal life was still unfulfilling. Then he met Paul Crane, by Winston's own description, "a corny white kid from Alabama."

"We hit it off real well," said Winston. "He was a linebacker. He always had corny jokes. He wasn't a playboy. He was what you'd call a square, I guess. Paul didn't have to drink to be in a good mood, yet he was always happy. He'd come to practice without a hangover while others of us just weren't up to going through the ordeal that day.

"He always had a good time, but he didn't stay up half the night to do it. And he always had a pretty girl with him—and a really nice girl, too. His language was clean. So I began to talk a lot with him and we shared a lot of time together. As we talked, he made me more aware of a lot of things. We didn't force anything on each other, but we had mutual respect and admiration for each other. He was very influential in getting my thinking about God back to where it ought to have been all along. It was then that I began to exercise my faith, as one would exercise his body. I began to grow as a Christian and developed more understanding about God and about myself. And I quit worrying about being accepted. It was a gradual process. Getting married and having two little girls really helped, too.

"I had been trying to get along with these heavy weights around my feet. I heard Dr. Hoffman speak about that one time, and he said that worrying about acceptance and succumbing to social pressures are like running with weights around our ankles.

Then God comes and snips these weights away. My responsibility is to him, not to society and not to any other human being. He may give us some heavy crosses to bear, but there is no experience a Christian cannot effectively deal with. The only thing that is really lasting is the Word of God. Everything else is just an experience, something that is going to pass away. No matter how good an experience is, it's going to pass away. You cannot retain it. But you can keep God forever.

"All God wants is for us to be happy. By exercising our faith, we give experiences back to God, and thereby open the way for him to give us more. He just keeps filling us up if we but put him first. It says in Psalm 23 that our cup will continue to run over, but not if we keep thinking only of material things. So many people think of freedom as being able to do anything, but it also means not having to do certain things because of different pressures."

Winston Hill believes a true Christian can feel himself being cleansed of sin. "We're cleansed through his blood and sacrifice" is the way he puts it. "When we accept his commitment, we can feel ourselves being cleansed. It's like washing clothes. The actual cleansing action is a wonderful thing. We can feel ourselves transforming, and we can feel some of the selfishness and greed going out of our hearts. And if we let him take over, we treat other people with more concern. We simply care more. You don't have to work hard at loving people. It's no struggle. It just comes naturally."

After fourteen seasons of football, that way of life has to be just about over for this towering lineman from East Texas. "Football is temporary," he said. "It's not lasting. I'll always be a Christian. I have committed my life to God. I don't know how I'll provide for my family, but I know God will show me a way. I'm excited about a lot of things—prison reform, counseling, marketing and sales, public speaking, social work, young people. I want to glorify God in everything that I do. I try to live the kind of life that will bring honor and glory to him.

"Like Paul, I can run close to the cliff and never slip, but my brother might not be so fortunate. A Christian can do anything. Whatever God asks me to do, I will do it. All he said was for us to have a little bit of faith and he'll help us exercise it. He promised us he'd give us talent and show us how to multiply it."

Hill speaks warmly of many of his teammates, past and present, and has special memories of an ex-Jet, Steve Thompson.

"He was really special," said Hill. "He finally quit football at the height of his career. He had a wife, two kids, and investments that had gone sour. But he just reached a crossroads with his faith and he asked himself if he could give up football. I guess he felt God was asking him if he could give it up—so he did.

"Steve and I talked a lot about meaningful things. When I was first married, I knew I had married a wonderful Christian girl, but I wanted her to make a few changes. Nothing major, mind you. So I asked Steve how I could get Carolyn to change a bit.

"He explained to me that God didn't send down a 'hatchet-man' to hit me on the head with a sledge hammer to work changes in me—he did it himself. And he said he didn't think God intended for me to try to work changes in my wife. He made me really think about it and I knew I was wrong."

Winston has warm praise for Joe Namath, his teammate of several years. "Joe's not the playboy he's made out to be. He's single and has girl friends. But he's not in love with himself. He's a very humble guy and treats people beautifully. He's not the person he's projected to be with the public. I've worked closely with him for several years at his football camp, and it's the best run camp in the country. Joe makes certain that every guy who's involved in running the camp with him is class all the way. He doesn't tolerate rowdies.

"Some people would have you believe that every night after camp Joe is out on the town. But instead of that, he gets into his boat and goes fishing. And I mean every night.

"After he closed his camp the final day of 1975, he got all the kids together and he spoke for thirty minutes. He told these young boys, 'Don't forget to thank God. Thank him for your health. Don't take it for granted. Get on your knees, and get into the habit of praying. He'll be there when you need him. And you'll find that the more you pray, you won't be asking him for *things*. Instead, you'll be thanking him for blessings he's given you.' "

Winston Hill calls that night one of the richest of his life.

11

The Toughest Kid in Town

All Ron Pritchard ever wanted out of life was recognition. Trouble is, he always wanted more than anyone else.

In the tough, mill town of Antioch, California, it took some doing to become recognized as the roughest kid in town. The best Ron Pritchard could do was to finish in a dead heat for first place.

He and Herbie Miles duked it out twice in one night, first at a high school dance then later at a drive-in. They were neither great friends nor mortal enemies. It was just that Herbie, a year older than Ron, was the state heavyweight wrestling champion and had gathered a pretty tough reputation around Antioch. Pritchard, the football hero, had his followers, too, and it was those followers who brought about the fights.

All they did was wonder, oft-times aloud, who'd come out on top in a scrap between Miles and Pritchard. Eventually, Miles and Pritchard began to wonder, too. And so it was that all the guesswork and wondering came to a head one night at a dance at the high school—the year Ron Pritchard graduated. They both had consumed too much beer, their friends had made too many boasts, and at the time, a fight seemed the only sensible solution.

Herbie weighed 220, Pritchard about 205. Herbie would out-muscle Ron, and Ron would outbox Herbie. The cops came before a winner could be determined. That left the two combatants and their supporters totally unsatisfied, if nearly exhausted.

They moved to a drive-in and word soon leaked back to Ron that Herbie had felt he gave better than he received. The only decent thing to do, Ron figured, was to have another go at it. So the battle resumed.

"It lasted at least ten minutes," Pritchard recalled one hot afternoon in the Cincinnati Bengals' training camp. "Now, ten minutes doesn't seem like a very long time, but it's an eternity when you're duking it out. Finally, as we were leaning on each

87

other against a car, we kind of looked at each other and figured there was just no sense in continuing."

To this day, there is no winner in the fight between the two. And to this day, no one has outfought Ron Pritchard although he's much more reluctant to square off.

"I'm sure there are lots of guys around who can take me," he said, "but it's just that I haven't run into them. Now, I don't want this to sound cocky because I'm trying to change all that, and I'm asking God each day to help me overcome this fault. I don't want to spend all my life proving myself."

"Proving" has been Ron Pritchard's big problem all along. He is a paradox, a strong, bull of a man ever willing, sometimes even eager, to stand and fight in order to gain acceptance.

He intimidated his peers from the time he was in junior high school. In college, he disdained the fraternity parties, preferring instead to be a part-time bouncer in a night club. Being tough simply was a way of life, and until recent years Ron Pritchard equated toughness only with his fists. Now, his goal is to become tougher emotionally and thus not have to prove anything physically.

"Life has always been a series of challenges for me," recalls the Bengals' linebacker. "Maybe I've looked for dares and challenges, I don't know. But I do know I've always found them. And it's always been really tough to turn away from them. It's just that I've never been able to gain control of my emotions.

"Someone challenges me and I get goofy. I just can't help it. It's a funny thing, though. I think I have a nice personality. I can mingle and I make friends easily. But I've always been a brawler. Maybe it's pride and respect. I've always had this great pride and I wanted respect more than anything else. I just wanted to be noticed, that's all. I've always tried to prove myself, and for the life of me I don't even know what I was trying to prove.

"Maybe it's the American system, to try and be the biggest and the best. For me, just participating isn't that much fun. I had to be the top dog. I'm not interested in being number two. It's always been all or nothing with me."

So consumed was Ron Pritchard with this idea that he neglected almost everything else in school. Mainly his studies. He nearly flunked out of high school.

Some fifty colleges and universities were so impressed by Pritchard's football credentials that they offered him scholarships. He chose Arizona State because of its rugged athletic reputation.

"I knew they had some real studs there, and I figured if I proved myself there, I'd be pretty happy about it."

His first year was marked by insecurity, yet he managed to win a starting position. By the time he reached his sophomore year, it occurred to him he was "pretty good."

"Some may define it as cocky, but I think I was just defensive," he recalls. "I didn't have a girl friend and I wasn't into the party scene. Football was everything to me. When a coach would get on me, I just didn't automatically back down. If I thought he was trying to make an example out of me, I'd strike back. One of the assistant coaches, Bob Owens, got on me and ordered me to run up a flight of stairs. Just to spite him, I refused. I told him if he didn't get off my back, I'd quit school and join a pro team. I even went so far as to tell him that my ability kept him working and made him look good. At the time, I thought that was pretty cool, but now I realize it was stupid and immature."

Pritchard had similar problems with his first pro team, the Houston Oilers, and later on with the Cincinnati Bengals.

"I was practically run out of Houston," he said. "They changed coaches so much no one knew what was going on. There was no stability, and I need stability. I just got frustrated. Lots of guys can handle that and roll with the situation, but not me. I get goofy when things are unsettled. So I said my piece and the coaches didn't like that. I got traded in the middle of the 1972 season. I didn't particularly want to come to Cincinnati and when I got here I figured I should be starting right away. But the Bengals had their system all set up and I wasn't starting, so I took it as a challenge and got hot under the collar again.

"I started ranting and raving at the coaching staff. My main target was Vince Costello and I screamed at him all the time. Now, he's a really beautiful man, and I look back on it as a shameful thing. But it goes back to my basic problem of not being able to control my emotions."

It is a curiosity that a bellicose, dukes-up brawler like Ron Pritchard was raised in a church-oriented home—but despite the fact he spent countless hours in church services, it was a belief he never really embraced.

His mother is a strong believer in a sect Ron finds too emotional for his tastes, and even today there is a rift in the family relationship because Ron's religious beliefs have taken a turn in another direction.

"I'm not knocking that church," Ron explained, "but it just

isn't for me. I remember saying to myself as a kid that I really wanted to be a Christian, but there was no way I could be in that kind of environment. I just couldn't do all the things that were expected of me. To me, they didn't preach the love that Jesus expressed when he died on the cross. I was taught that God is a punishing kind of God. It was built around holiness and doctrine was placed above salvation.

"Even as a kid I didn't want to go to church, but I was forced to go. I realized I couldn't be a Christian in their eyes. I wanted to be honest. I didn't want to live a phony life. I guess I was in the ninth or tenth grade when I decided to break away from it. I couldn't hack it. It's as simple as that. I believed in God, but I didn't know anything about salvation, and organized religion, as I knew it, turned me off."

At Arizona State, Ron Pritchard became acquainted with marijuana and pep pills and paid little or no attention to God. He got his attention through football and fighting.

He got more attention once he graduated into the pro football ranks, not just as a fine linebacker but as a wrestler as well. "The opportunity came along to be on the pro wrestling circuit," he said, and I took it. It helped me financially for quite a while and it was all right for a time. After five years, though, I couldn't take it any longer. It's a bizarre world, and I mean really bizarre. There are just too many opportunities to get into trouble. You're away from home a lot. It just got to be too much for me to handle emotionally. It was really a cut-throat world and it's against every principle God talks about. I wasn't strong enough to be any kind of disciple in that world, and God showed me a way to get out of it. I was projecting a lie. I was billed as a clean-cut-American type young man . . . the good guy and all that . . . but it was a lousy environment for me and I had to escape it."

Ron Pritchard would never have been interested in escaping from that bizarre world, nor interested in calming his hair-trigger temper, nor in controlling his emotions, nor in curbing his swearing, had it not been for a conference of Christian pro football players after the 1972 season.

Pritchard went more out of curiosity than anything else. He knew a lot of top performers would be there and it was a chance to bask in the sun for a few days. He figured on attending a session or two, but mainly the purpose of the trip was the sun and the sand. He tells what happened.

"At the conference I was the guy sticking out like a sore

thumb. I had gotten into the chapel services once in a while when I was with the Oilers, but I really wasn't dedicated to the whole idea. And I was mixed up. I remember when I was little, I thought God would use me as a preacher. Then I fell away. When I went to the conference, I didn't know whether I was fish or fowl. Maybe I was searching, or just looking for another challenge, I really don't know. But I think everyone there figured I would be disruptive.

"But all of a sudden in one of the sessions, I got up from my seat and began to cry. I was going to be witty and all that, but I couldn't even speak., I couldn't do anything but stand there anu cry. The whole place was quiet except for some other guys crying. It was a little embarrassing at first, but I knew in my heart that I had finally accepted Christ, and on his terms. Every time I stand up to witness in a service now, I cry all over again. I just can't help it, it's such an emotional thing.

"Rededicating my life to Christ didn't solve all my problems nor get rid of all the pain and suffering in my life. God never promised us that. On the contrary, he told us we'd be persecuted and tested constantly for his sake. I believe it's harder to be a Christian than a non-Christian, but look at the rewards for being one! I think God puts us through trials and tribulations in order to mold us into what he wants us to be. He has saved me, but my mother thinks my beliefs are really off-base. But I know God will take care of everything if I just let him lead and direct my path. Part of the great commission that the Lord laid out for us is that we are all disciples—now we're not all apostles and we don't all have the stature of a Billy Graham—but in our own small ways we are disciples.

"It's an odd thing, you know—when I went to that conference, it was a total mix-up in my head. I knew about God, and I wanted to know a lot more about him. But I was certain I didn't want to bring him into my life. There were too many other things I wanted to do first. But come to find out, I couldn't do anything with my life until I had turned it over to him. All this time I had been worried about what man expected of me, never giving any real thought to what God expected of me."

The conference was arranged by Dr. Ira Lee Eshleman, the same "chaplain to the pros" who had helped light the way for Charlie Sanders of the Detroit Lions.

His is a simple message: That salvation is a gift from God and that if we but accept his love and his way, we can begin a new life. Ron Pritchard had been concerned about "righteousness" and not about salvation. He had been thoroughly confused by his early teachings, even embarrassed by that method of worship.

"I don't know what's the right way and what are the wrong ways," he added, "but I do know what works for me. The church I grew up in places a great deal of emphasis on being filled with the Holy Ghost and about speaking in tongues. Now, I know the Bible speaks of that in several places, but the whole thing is not completely clear to me. I was taught that if a person is really with it all the way, then God will give him a special gift—speaking in tongues.

"My wife Claudia has always been a good moral person, and she thought she had accepted Christ—but since I got to know him in a very personal way she, too, has rededicated herself to Jesus. And it's made our marriage and our life together much more complete.

"More than once we've gotten down on our knees and prayed to God about this business of tongues. Neither of us understands it, but we've told God 'If this thing is for the true believers, don't leave us out.' So we're just waiting on the Lord, for him to give us direction and guidance. There's so much we don't understand, but we keep searching God's Word and believing that he'll tell us what we should do.

"When I pray, I ask him to forgive me for all the things I'm doing wrong, and for the things I fail to do in his behalf. I know what they are, and I name them one by one. I want God to make an example out of me, and even though it's difficult sometimes, I thank God for my tribulation.

"When I prayed at the conference, it was a begging kind of prayer. I remember saying 'Lord, please come into my life and make me a new person. I'm miserable anyway and I need help.'

"Before a game, I pray that if it be God's will, I will play very well. I pray for my family to be safe, and for all the people in the stands to know God. I pray that no one will be hurt and that I will be able to stand all the punishment of the game. I just want to do my very best, and then give God the glory."

Ron Pritchard used to pray to be named to the all-pro team but those days are behind him now. He is especially fond of the same verse the author's father uttered just before his death: "Not that I speak in respect of want, for I have learned, in whatsoever state I am therewith to be content" (Phil. 4:11).

Since he accepted Christ, he worries less about whether he is accepted by his peers. "My life has taken on a whole new meaning. I'm involved with my family in a church life at the Baptist Church in Sharpstown, Texas. We have a prayer group once a week and I'm into the Bible every night. I pray that I'll become a good example and that I may have some influence on others.

"I want to be able to control my emotions better. You know, Jesus Christ was the strongest person—emotionally—in history. He had control of it all. He had command of the whole show. He got angry, but he didn't sin. He had that kind of control. He was tempted, but he had control. He felt scorn and rejection and disappointment, but he had control.

"Jesus showed me the way out of wrestling and he's showing me the way out of swearing and he's showing me how to have more control in my life. At first, I was uncomfortable witnessing for him, but he's showing me the way to do that. He's giving me more respect for others' feelings and their points of view.

"He has tested all the great Christians and asked tremendous sacrifices at times. I pray that whatever he asks of me I'll be able to do it and not ever question his wisdom. I think of him as a lonely and jealous God. When I was taking 'uppers'—and I took them for ten years—I felt I needed some extra energy to do my job in football. But since God took over my life, I get my energy from him. I just don't need any pills, and I'm a better football player without them.

"As for being challenged physically, I'm probably not at the point yet where I can turn the other cheek all the time. I'd like to be able to say 'Hey, God loves you and I love you and I'll see you later.' But I'm not there yet, but with God's help, I'll make it someday. When I was in the ninth grade, I told myself I'd never back away from a fight and that's the worst promise I ever made to myself.

"It's like being the fastest gun in the West. The fastest gun always has to prove himself and eventually there's a faster gun somewhere and you're gone. I think being in the National Football League has helped, too. After all, it's a physical thing, and there are only about a thousand guys who are good enough to make it. And I'm one of them.

"I'm not competing with my neighbor for anything. I don't have to have the biggest house nor the biggest car. I don't care about having a boat or a membership in the finest country club.

I want to have my family safe and well cared for. I think a lot about the Apostle Paul. He had known good times and bad, and he could handle either one because of the grace of God. Without God, he was nothing. With God, he learned that all things are possible.

"He's given me and my wife a beautiful love between ourselves. He's given us two beautiful children, Gia and Cole. They have a beautiful, pure love for us—like the love God has for all of his children. I believe God wants us to love him as our children love us. When I first invited him into my life and I knew he was actually living in me, there was a tremendous high. And it never stops, you know. It's a wonderful feeling, knowing that through Jesus Christ who died for our sins, I'm going to live forever."

Terry Bradshaw
Pittsburgh Steelers

Roger Staubach, Dallas Cowboys

Right: Don Cockroft
Cleveland Browns

Below: Craig Clemons
Chicago Bears

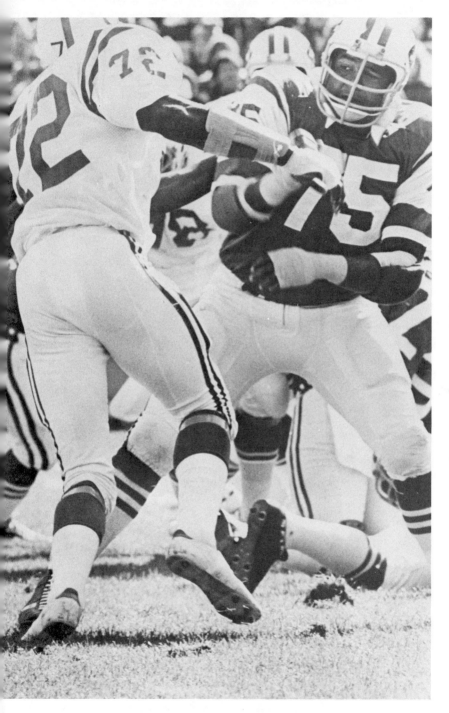

Winston Hill, New York Jets

Ron Pritchard
Cincinnati Bengals

Paul Krause (holding), Fred Cox (kicking), Minnesota Vikings

Charlie Sanders
Detroit Lions

Merlin Olsen
Los Angeles Rams

Right: Harold Jackson
Los Angeles Rams

Below: Steve Owens
Detroit Lions

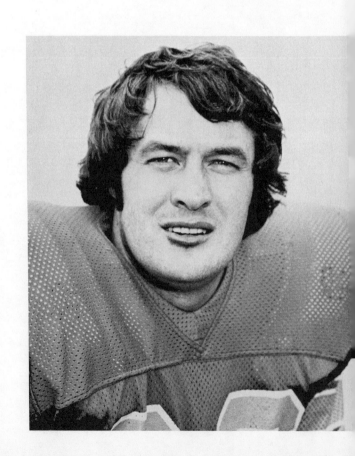

Jeff Siemon, Minnesota Vikings

"Doc" Eshleman discusses with President Gerald Ford
how Christian football players can have a spiritual impact on America

12

A Light from Heaven

John Small remembers the night very well. There was a chill in the air. A light fog was hanging over the stadium. It was late in the first period of the game between his Citadel team and Chattanooga.

The Citadel was getting whipped—as The Citadel usually does in sports. But John was having another good game. After one period, he already had eleven tackles. But that was not uncommon, since he was the outstanding defensive player on the squad and since the defense was on the field most of the time. He generally wound up with some twenty tackles each game, and even though he would not be available for the professional football draft for a couple of seasons, John was already being noticed by the pro scouts.

Toward the end of the first half he went to make another tackle and found himself on the ground, paralyzed from the waist up. Teammates rushed to the stricken player. The team trainer and the doctor could do nothing. John Small was unable to move. Earlier, he had suffered a neck injury and he was fearful that this time he had broken his neck.

The date was October 24, 1968, and John Small remembers it as clearly as if it happened last night. "I just looked up to the heavens, and I realized that everything about my life was wrong. I was going nowhere. I had no purpose, no direction to my life. I wasn't happy and fulfilled. So I just looked up and turned my life over to Jesus Christ. I asked him to help me, to alter my life, and to use me in whatever way he wanted. It was really just a simple matter of confessing my sins and making Jesus Christ my pilot and letting him steer my ship of life. Since that night, Jesus has been the central figure in my life. When I turned things over to him, I did it for keeps. And whatever my lot, I know he loves me and I know he watches over me."

John Small recovered from that injury. Even though he had

to be carried from the field on a stretcher he was hospitalized only for one night. He played the following Saturday. Five times during his college and professional career, he has gone under the surgeon's knife and five times he has come back and tried to win a place in football. It has been a struggle that a lesser man might have forsaken.

"I'm still working at it," he said, as he watched other members of the Detroit Lions prepare for the final few games of the 1975 campaign. It was another season John Small had spent with doctors and surgeons and trainers because of injuries. "God still hasn't taken the desire to play football out of my heart. I still want to play and I won't give up until he takes the desire away from me. When the desire is gone, then I'll give up the fight."

Small is persuaded that without a Spirit-filled life, he could never muster the courage to shake off so many operations and battle such staggering odds to reestablish his professional career.

"Look," he cautioned, "I know the Word. And I know that through Jesus all things are possible. He gave up his life for me, and he had more courage than anyone in history. It doesn't require a lot of me to hang in there through these setbacks."

John Small never looks upon the surgeries (four on his knees, one on his neck) as anything but challenges. As early as his junior high school days, he was advised by doctors to give up playing football. Five operations later he is still ignoring their suggestions. His logic is that if God wanted him to give up football, then God would take the desire out of him.

Athletic competition was an outlet, an escape for a young John Small. Son of a career army man who moved his brood around from North Carolina to California to Newfoundland to Oklahoma to Texas to Georgia, John learned two things: To pack quickly and to make new friends easily.

Times were tough. The environment was transient. "We were always poor. My folks were good people and I was pretty happy, but I had no real inner peace. My whole life was wrapped up in sports. I could do everything. I could hit a baseball further, throw it better—you name it, I could do it. I knew I was better than average and for as long as I can remember, I somehow knew if I was going to make anything out of myself and provide a better environment for myself and escape from the poverty I was accustomed to, I'd have to do it through sports. And truthfully, that's all I thought of. I was consumed by it. I can't tell you how much drive I had to succeed.

"But until the night back in 1968 when I accepted Jesus as my personal Savior, I was an empty person. There was an uncertainty about me that was eating me up inside. I was just plain corrupt. I'm not saying I went around robbing people or drinking heavily or anything like that, but I was a self-centered person. I didn't think of anyone but John Small. I didn't like anyone and at the time I didn't understand that I couldn't like anyone because I didn't like myself.

"I was one mean hombre. I'd fight at the drop of a hat. I didn't trust anyone. I went to all the right parties with all the rich kids. I didn't have a dime but I was allowed into that circle because I was a top jock when I was in high school in Augusta, Georgia. Right up until that night on the football field in Chattanooga, I wasn't a happy person and I didn't have the capacity to make anyone else happy.

"I was just missing out on everything important in life. Here, I had been all-everything in high school and had gotten tremendous honors. At the Citadel, I got one rave notice after another. Here I was, a big football hero, and down deep inside I was really nothing. There was a tremendous void in my life that couldn't be filled by awards, trophies, honors, and press clippings. But when I permitted Christ to come into my life, he gave me purpose, direction, and peace. He took away the volcano that was erupting all the time, and gave me a love for my fellow man. Suddenly the hostility was gone.

"There's an old gospel song entitled, 'I Saw the Light.' Well, let me tell you, I saw it. I love to read about Paul. You know, he saw a light from heaven. He had to be struck blind before he got himself together. It was the same way with me. My father had taught me at an early age that if I couldn't whip someone with my fists that I should go get a stick. And that's the way I lived. That's the way my mind worked. If someone said something to me, I always took it the wrong way. I'd look for the worst in people and in situations, never the best. I'd invariably take out my own frustrations and unhappiness on other people. But Christ changed all that."

Today, John and Lucia Small have a happy, secure life that is God-centered, because—the way John puts it—he found that Jesus Christ was the missing piece in his puzzle. Small feels it was almost preordained that he would find Christ—or that Christ would find him—on the football field because up until that time, that's where his whole life was centered.

They are deeply involved in a youth program back in Augusta during the off-season, they concentrate heavily on a Bible study program involving other football players and their wives, and they're wrapped up in activities at the Calvary Baptist Church of Hazel Park, Michigan. John is an exuberant, demonstrative Christian who sings aloud his praises of Christ.

"I just can't help it," he said. "I realize that maybe sometimes I turn people off with my enthusiasm and I try to guard against it. There are saved people and there are unsaved people, and I know the unsaved are like I was. Sometimes being confronted with the message of Christ makes them uncomfortable. I know it used to make me squirm.

"But I've found the best way to behave is to act normally. And for me, being normal is being a Christian. Some people may think I'm hyper about Jesus, but I'm just being me. He made me a new person. He gave me a new life. I'm born again. And hopefully, my example, and the happiness and the peace of mind that radiates from me will reach out and touch others. Christ has given us specific instructions on the way we are supposed to live. We're all to be evangelists, and we're all to carry his message to others.

"When I was unsaved, I persecuted people and put them down—just like Paul did. And like I tell people when I speak to groups all around the country, I was a hellacious person. I was living like hell, and it took something like lying there paralyzed on the football field to get the hell scared out of me.

"Christ had to appear to Paul and ask why Paul was persecuting him. And that's what finally changed Paul's life. The same Christ who changed Paul's life changed mine, and he can change everyone else's life, too. So that's why I shout it from the rooftops, because Jesus Christ hung on the cross for me. Every time I think about him dying for me, I break out in chill bumps. I'm a bondservant of Christ. You see, I have come back to slavery, except now I'm not a slave of sin, but a slave of Jesus Christ. He's my Master, and I will spend my life serving him."

John tells how he examined other faiths and denominations and attended many different kinds of church services:

"I looked at all of them—just about every Protestant church you can name and the Catholic Church, too. Finally I found two church homes, the one here in Michigan and the One Way Baptist Church in Augusta. I think that's a heckuva name—One Way—because you know, there's just one way, and it's his way. All through my young life, I never got to know anyone who really followed Jesus in such a way as to give me a living example of a God-filled life. I'm just thankful for that night on the football field. And I found Christ not by any good works I had done, because it's for sure I hadn't done any. I was saved by grace."

The Smalls have daily prayer sessions in their home and John always has his Bible with him during practice and at games during the football season.

"I just don't think you can grow as a Christian without a continuous study of God's Word," he advised. "Dr. David D. Allen of our church in Michigan and Eddie West down in Augusta are Bible students, and I have learned a tremendous amount of Scripture from both of them. To know the Word of God is to find direction in your life. You can't find the way to peace and happiness without a road map, and the Bible is the road map. That's all there is to it. I don't understand all that's in the Bible and maybe no one else does either, but the answers to every man's problems are in there. All we have to do is search the Word."

John finds more and more professional football players receptive to the Christian way of life. The chapel sessions each team has prior to the games and the weekly Bible study groups have had significant growth. During the off-season there are several seminars and conferences that find pro players sharing their experiences with each other, and with high school athletes as well.

Much of Small's off-season energies are devoted to a program in Augusta called "The First Step." It was started several years ago by Small and some associates who work with troubled teenagers.

"We take kids off the street," said John. "We have kids with drug problems, girls who've gotten into trouble, kids from broken homes, all sorts. We provide entertainment for them, counsel with them, and share the Bible with them. Oft-times we get jobs for them.

"Some are poor and don't get enough food, so we try to take care of that. We're trying to raise funds throughout the country—we're a non-profit outfit—but there's a terrific amount of work to be done and at the same time a tremendous amount of good that can be accomplished. We like to think we can provide young people with the first step toward the good life. If we can get 'em on the right track, they have a good chance to stay there. Young people need love, they need to know they're wanted, that they're important, that someone cares. Hopefully, it'll be a full-time job for me when I'm all done with football."

Again, doctors have told Small he should give up football. "But God hasn't told me that yet," he reminded. "I'm thankful he's given Lucia and me three wonderful children. We have a home that's filled with Christian love. My wife understands my love for the game of football, and I just think football gives me so much more than just the resources to provide well for my family. It gives me a platform from which I can speak about Jesus Christ and from which hopefully I can reach a whole lot of people who are living like I was. If I can help one other person find Jesus Christ and through him achieve a purpose and a meaning to life, then my life will have been well spent."

Most of us have special or meaningful passages of Scripture. For John Small, it is "For I am not ashamed of the gospel of Christ: for it is the power of God unto salvation to every one that believeth; to the Jew first, and also to the Greek" (Rom. 1:16).

He also is particularly fond of Philippians 3:14, "I press toward the mark for the prize of the high calling of God in Christ Jesus."

When John Small returned to the Detroit Lions from his fifth encounter with the surgeon, some people expressed shock that he would give the pro game one more effort.

"One guy looked me right in the eye and said 'John, you know you're crazy.' I know I'm crazy, but I'm crazy about Jesus Christ. These adversities are nothing! They're just challenges that I must overcome. If I quit now, I'd be doing myself and Christ an injustice. If he wants me to stay in football, he'll keep the door open for me."

Not since 1972 has John Small played an entire season, but he has the distinction of having performed at seven different positions during his checkered professional career.

Not since a chilly, foggy October night in 1968 in Chattanooga, Tennessee, has he understood the meaning of the word "quit."

13

Stand Up and Be Counted

In 1970, rebellion on the American college campus was commonplace. Students were staging riots, burning ROTC buildings, protesting against the war in Vietnam and asserting themselves as individuals more than ever before. The black man, in his continuing struggle for equality, was being more assertive.

Calvin Jones understood neither the war nor the social injustices. If his world consisted merely of batted down passes and open field tackles, those things might not have mattered. But it was not enough for him to be just a football star on his college team. He had grown up in an "involved" family, and it was his nature to be concerned about the world in which he was living.

Besides, Calvin Jones had made a brand new commitment to Jesus Christ in 1969. It was this commitment to Christ that compelled him to take a bold stand in a major racial issue the following year.

As a sophomore at the University of Washington, Jones quickly became a star defensive back. He was so good, in fact, that he was named to the all-Pacific Eight Conference defensive team and mentioned for all-America honors. Of the fifty-five players on the Washington varsity football squad, sixteen or seventeen were black players. Only Jones was a starter.

There had been rumblings the year before among the black athletes. Among themselves, they figured the coaching staff was "stacking" the black players—in other words, if there were seven receivers on the squad, three white receivers would compete for the job on the left side of the line and the four black receivers would be stacked against each other on the right side. Stacking insured there'd be a limited number of black starters on the team.

The University of Washington team finished the 1970 campaign with a 6–4 record. After the season was over, the four black athletes who would have returned to the squad the following season quit the team. Along with their boycott, they issued a statement accusing the university coaching staff of practicing racial discrimination. Quickly, the attentions of the sports world were focused on Seattle, Washington. National magazines wrote articles about the situation. The story was distributed on national television. Columnists had a field day.

For Calvin Jones, it was the first major test of his faith as a Christian and his stature as a man. "A lot of people came down on me," Calvin recalled. "The press intimated that I was pressured into joining the boycott and that I had been intimidated by black militants and off-campus groups. Some folks said the other players talked me into it and suggested I was being used because I was the only black starter.

"The truth is that many, many players came to me and urged me not to take part. They said since I was a starter, and since I had two years of eligibility left, that by joining the boycott I'd be jeopardizing my career. They encouraged me to keep out of it and stay on at the university.

"But I couldn't do that and remain a man. I was fully aware of what was going on. It had been going on before I came to the university. The practice of stacking was just one of the things that was wrong. I'm not saying I am the greatest judge of football talent, but I know there were skilled blacks who should have been starting. And there were still others who should have been getting more playing time.

"For example, we really needed a breakaway runner. We had Sonny Sixkiller as our quarterback and all we really needed to balance our attack was a good outside running threat. A black player by the name of Herman Houston definitely had the style we needed, but he didn't get to play much. One of the coaches shrugged it off by saying that wasn't the University of Washington's style.

"The black players didn't put the blame on head coach Jim Owens, but directed it mainly on some of the assistant coaches. However when we came out with our statement, naturally the blame had to be put on the doorstep of the head coach because he's the guy who's responsible for getting the best talent on the field. And the fact was—a lot of the time we had the best talent sitting on the bench."

Once the boycott was on, the statement issued, and the battle lines drawn, the frustrations mounted. Jones said part of his world came tumbling down:

"I guess the thing that bothered me most—and still bothers me—is that many people who profess to be Christians came down hardest on me. They said I wasn't being a Christian. But down deep inside me, I actually felt God was leading me to make that move. I can't say that I expected Christians everywhere to rise up in a group and get behind me, but I did expect them to understand why I was doing what I was doing.

"I certainly didn't anticipate the flak I got from people who described themselves as Christians and then accused me of being totally non-Christian. I got a lot of nasty letters. But when I examined the Scriptures and read the story again about the Good Samaritan, I understood there was bigotry in Christ's time just as there is now. And I realized I had to really show love, and not bitterness and hatred.

"It occurred to me that my college football days were over, and if not, I'd have to transfer to a smaller school. I thought about the possibility I'd be black-listed and branded as a trouble-maker. If I ever had any aspirations to a career in professional football, I took a chance on those hopes being washed away. But I knew in my heart I just had to stand up and be counted. To me, it was a completely Christian thing to do."

Calvin Jones was a brand new bridegroom at about that time. He and Marlene Regina Peterson had been married the August before his sophomore season.

"We had gone to junior high school and high school together," he said. "We found out we were born in the same hospital, and we lived only about ten minutes apart while we were growing up. But we never dated until I left high school and went away to college. She wrote to me while I was in college, and she'd send me chocolate chip cookies—my very favorite kind—and that's how we got together."

By leaving the University of Washington voluntarily, Calvin gave up his scholarship. He and Marlene headed for Long Beach where he enrolled in another school. He planned to get sufficient credits in order to play football at Long Beach State.

Back up the Pacific coast, the turmoil at the university was increasing. The president of the school appointed a human rights commission to probe the allegations of discriminatory practices. Seattle newspapers wrote articles, the investigatory kind. *Sports Illustrated* trained its guns on the problems at the University of Washington.

Jones and the other players had met with the school's board

of regents and detailed their complaints. One player had secretly taped a conversation with one of the assistant coaches and it smacked of racism. The human rights commission—made up of blacks, whites, militants, conservatives, you name it—finally concluded there was, indeed, racism in the school's athletic program. The commission recommended the head coach be fired.

"I was never that hung up on Coach Owens being a racist," said Jones. "He's really aloof from his players, white and black. The players just never got to know him that well because he's not the kind of guy who lets his players get too close to him. As for the discrimination, some white guys were aware of it, too, and were really hung up on it.

"About six months after the big blowup, I got a call at Long Beach State from one of the coaches at Washington. The old school had hired a black assistant athletic director, a black assistant coach, a black baseball coach, and some black secretaries in the athletic department. The coach asked me if I'd like to apologize and come back to Washington. I told him I wanted to return, but that I didn't feel I had done anything wrong and so I didn't see the need to make any kind of an apology.

"Then, just one week before it was time to start practice in August, Don Smith, who had been hired as the black assistant athletic director, called and urged me to come back. He assured me an apology wouldn't be necessary. He told me I could make any kind of statement I wanted to make to the press, and that I wouldn't be muzzled. All that was needed was for me and Coach Owens to agree on my coming back."

So there was a meeting in Los Angeles, involving the player, the coach, the assistant athletic director, and Calvin Jones' attorney. From that came an understanding, a handshake, and the return of a scintillating athlete to the campus where he had wanted to be all along.

"Going back was beautiful," said Jones. "The white players really understood what was going on. They were great to me. The black guys weren't looking for any kind of quota. All we wanted was quality. We wanted to win, just like everyone else. There was no pressure at all when I went back. There was a more aggressive recruitment of black players. Everything was in focus for the first time.

"I don't even know how many blacks we had on the team when I went back. There were a couple of freshmen who came in, and three or four other guys who tried out. But the important thing is, everyone played better. It was a complete new program. The problems were behind us and the atmosphere was bright and enjoyable. And in my last two seasons, the team went 8–3 each year. We were not only a good team, we were a together team."

And what does he think of Coach Owens today?

"I respect him as a man, and I respect him for helping to effect a compromise. I have no hostility at all toward him. I respect him for making the effort he did."

It was really a compromise that brought Calvin to the University of Washington in the first place. He had been an athletic star at Balboa High School in San Francisco. The Reverend Calvin Jones, Sr., was the minister of a large Baptist church in the city. He and his wife had three children—Nathaniel, Calvin, and Brenda Jean.

Besides being a sports star in high school, Calvin also had been elected president of the student body. Either his citizenship or his athletic ability could have gotten him a college scholarship. He explained: "A college up in Maine wanted me to come up there and I didn't have to play football, but I guess I didn't want to go that far away from home. Besides, I wanted to see if I could make it in football at a big school. I could have gone to Indiana or to schools in the Bay area, however, I chose Washington because it was away from home, but yet not too far.

"It was a difficult time in my life. I was struggling to become a young man. I was just trying to declare my individuality. I had accepted Jesus Christ and had been baptized when I was nine years old, but I had been living a lie, really. When things were going well in sports and at school, the girls were around, and I thought life was good. In my senior year, I banged up my knee and got scared a little bit, so I started praying. I told God I'd promise to quit staying out late, I'd pray more, and study the Bible and go to church more if he'd just let me somehow get a scholarship. I got it, but then I put God right back in the closet.

"My parents and I weren't getting along very well. We were having trouble communicating like lots of people do at that stage in life. So I was anxious to get away to college. I went up to the University of Washington before school started and got a job working from three-to-midnight. I worked that whole summer and did a lot of thinking. I started reading the Bible all over again.

"But I was really hung up about the war in Vietnam and about the social problems in the United States. I had read all the history about World War II, and it seemed like a just war. But this thing in Vietnam seemed ridiculous. We didn't really want to win it. It seemed like a big game to me. So I got involved in a lot of campus activities. I went out and demonstrated against the things I thought were wrong.

"Then one night I went to the library to study. But instead of studying what I should have been working on, I was reading the San Francisco newspapers and I spotted a picture. It was a picture of the peace talks going on in Paris, and all these people from the various nations had been sitting around trying to solve the problems of the world. One guy just got up and walked out of the meeting, and the caption said he walked out because he was offended.

"I just couldn't believe it. Here's a guy who should be sitting there trying to work out a peace agreement, and he stalked out because his feelings were hurt. People were being killed right and left, and he's not even trying to stop it. And that kind of represented me right about that time. Here I was, running around trying to save the world, but my own life was still fouled up. I was ashamed of myself.

"Right then I made up my mind that there had to be a change in my life. And I said, 'God, if you're real, come into my life right now, and change it.' And that's when Christ became a living reality for me. That's when I got him out of the closet for good. I went home to my dormitory room on the sixth floor at Terry Hall, and I sat down on my bed and prayed. I was just eighteen years old and a freshman in college. Finally I had really committed my life to Jesus Christ. Then I discovered I really didn't need my individuality.

"That's when I started reading the Word, and studying the Bible, and understanding that we've had political, social, and economic turmoil since the beginning of time and that Christ had to deal with those things. I learned that man's purpose is to follow Christ. At that point I started to really appreciate my parents, and I began to get answers to a lot of the questions that had been in my mind. I don't have the answers to solve all the problems that come along, but at least I know why things happen now. I understood for the first time that Christ can deal with all the world's problems in a real and lasting way if man will let him.

"Here I was spouting off about racism, and I can't honestly say that I've been without racist feelings. I don't think any one can say he's totally clean of that. It takes time. We are a racist society, and until we accept Christ, and put him first, we can't eliminate discrimination. There are problems all over the world, in the Middle East, in Ireland—you name it—even though we call ourselves a Christian nation, and even though the Word of God has been spread throughout all lands, we will not solve our problems until the world puts him first. We have to make a total commitment to him, and understand what he demands of us. He commands us to love one another, and right now, we don't."

Calvin Jones feels Christians too often give money instead of themselves. And it has been written that we truly give only when we give of ourselves.

"I still have to check myself out when I'm speaking to white congregations about the racial problems," he said, "to make sure I'm together in my thinking. Too many professing Christians prostitute Christ by making the Bible say what they want it to say. For centuries, men have tried to own other men. Men have killed other men in the name of Christianity. I love that part of the Bible that admonishes us about hatred . . . you know, Jesus challenged people severely when he asked them how they could say they loved God, whom they had not seen, when they go around hating their brothers, whom they have seen.

"Sure, there's still discrimination in a lot of places, and some of it is being carried out by people who otherwise are really lovers of God. It's just that they haven't been able to get it all straightened out yet. But with God's help, they will.

"He is the hope of the world, you know. We can have different cultures and languages and circumstances, but through the love of Christ we can all communicate in a common way. Christ gives us the power to overcome Satan. Christ enables us to deal with the bad things that crop up in our lives. He knows we cannot be perfect, but we should strive for perfection, as it is written in the Word."

Calvin Jones is only 5–7 and weighs 175 (if he puts some wet sand in his socks). Physically, he has no business playing football anywhere, particularly in the National Football League. The Denver Broncos, by making him their fifteenth round draft choice after his graduation from Washington, conceded only that he deserved a brief look–see. Opposing runners and pass-catchers have been looking at Calvin ever since.

"Every time I look at those big guys in the league," he says, "and each time I screen the films of our games, I wonder my-self what I'm doing out there. I really do. It's my testimony, I guess."

His professional ambition, naturally, is to play on a champion-ship team in Denver, even though he believes the world is too hung up on this thing we call success: "I think our whole society has trouble with it. We've almost made a religion out of success. Even in school, we've had the good students seated in the front, the average students in the middle and the inferior students in the rear. We make a terrible distinction between winners and losers, and I'm not at all sure it's totally healthy. If a person flunks the bar exams or the medical boards, we brand him a loser. I hope we can get to the point in our society where we are content with people who give their best, who contribute 100 percent all the time. I think that makes a man successful.

"People have asked me if I pray for success in football, and the answer I give them is that I'm not at all sure God cares whether I look good in a game or if the Denver Broncos win. I feel what he wants is for each of us to play to maximum poten-tial. I think he wants us to glorify him in all that we do. He can use people like us to influence others. I'm not suggesting my career in professional football is a Christian calling, but I do enjoy it, and I know that God gave me the ability to play this game.

"First of all, I enjoy the game. But playing it and being a Christian doesn't mean that Calvin Jones is going to convert a bunch of football fans every weekend. It means, though, that my relationship with the people gives me a chance to share Christ, an opportunity to say publicly that Jesus Christ has blessed me, and to tell the world that Jesus Christ is a living, practical bless-ing in my life.

"You know, Christ told his disciples in the last verses of Mat-thew 28 to spread his gospel throughout the world. We must share him with others. We are put in situations all the time where we can share Christ. Too often, I think Christians have held a sort of condescending attitude toward non-Christians. Too many times we've treated them like second-class citizens, like they really don't belong in our cozy little world. But now I believe Christians are becoming more aware of their responsibilities, and more Christians now know they must demonstrate for others how Christ has dramatically changed their lives.

"I've been reading an article about sinners and Christians and it makes a lot of good sense. I found salvation through knowing Jesus Christ, and as a believer, I have made a commitment to Jesus Christ. That doesn't necessarily make me better than the next guy. That doesn't put me on a better plateau. That doesn't mean I'm good all of a sudden, and that everyone else is beneath me. If we dare compare ourselves to him, we find we're just rags. It's really exciting for me to know that as Christians, our power source is the Holy Spirit. You know, he said we'd do great works in his name. I think he is telling us that if we believe and follow in the light, we can do as many good works in his name as our faith will allow. But to do those things, you have to be plugged into the Holy Spirit."

The word around the National Football League is that Calvin Jones has had a profound influence on other athletes.

"If that's true, then I praise God for it," he said. "But I've had hard times, too. The Bible talks about God and his grace and says the spirit will be with us at all times once we accept Jesus. But nowhere does it say we won't have problems and temptations. Christ himself was tempted.

"In this world, it's easy to become tempted and confused. Sometimes we sort of blend in with the world, because the world is a pretty sinful place and we go along with things just because something is a normal and accepted practice, even if it's wrong. The South is supposed to be the Bible Belt, but there's a lot of hatred there among both whites and blacks for each other. When you see this sort of thing, you have to question if the values of this country are more important than the values of the command of God that we love one another. We're supposed to love our brothers as we love ourselves—that's the basis of the Christian faith as I see it—and when we don't have that love between the races or between the classes, I think we have to question the reality of our relationship with God.

"I believe in the parable of the talents, and I know God wants me to share my faith and my talent. If this mark that the world calls success is upon Calvin Jones, then Calvin Jones has to do something with it, rather than sit around doing nothing. The excitement of knowing Jesus Christ is something I just have to share with others. Without Jesus Christ, Marlene and I might not have made it. But we've made him the center of our relationship, and we have that firm foundation that has enabled us to weather all the storms.

"We both still have our temptations, and I have taken her for granted a lot of times and it's been tense once in a while. But God didn't make a mistake in putting us together. The mistakes have been ours. But we know what Christ expects of us, and we are committed not just to each other, but to him."

When he's not playing football, Calvin Jones is learning the ropes of the radio business and in his spare time is going around sharing his testimony with others. He particularly likes the challenge of addressing himself to the teen-aged audiences.

"I think they can identify with me," he explained. "I grew up in a town where I had all the temptations. I could have gone in either direction, good or bad. I don't know if the church today has failed in its mission to the young people, if it hasn't related to their problems, or what, but young people have so many temptations it's almost unbelievable.

"I try to point out to them that Jesus Christ is the only sensible alternative to these other things, that he offers them something meaningful and lasting and beautiful—something that can give them life eternal. I try not to emphasize the do-and-don't part of it. Rather, I focus on the personality of Jesus Christ, and what he offers us. He is the hope of the world. All we have to do is work a little harder to get this great message out to people in a new and unique way.

"The message isn't simply that Christ *was*—but that he *is*—and that he will be forever."

14

The Winners on God's Team

Paul Krause was not suggesting that God takes special care of the Minnesota Vikings because there are so many committed Christians on the Minnesota football team. After all, God loves everyone, and there are Christians on every team in the National Football League.

But it is the belief of the veteran defensive back that one of the major reasons the Minnesota Vikings have been so successful over the years is that they are a happy, unified group of athletes.

"We have outstanding human beings on our team," said Krause. "We have good character on the squad and I'm sure that's one of the major factors in our winning. We have no friction, spiritually or otherwise. We have a dozen to fifteen players who regularly attend our chapel services on Sundays. We have the same number of players and their wives who come together on Wednesday nights for Bible study—and this has been a truly great thing for our players.

"And now we've invited athletes from other professional teams in the Twin Cities to meet with us, and people from the Twins and North Stars are joining us. As for our football team, it's a wonderful thing the way we are together as a unit. It's tough for any group of some forty men to join together and have that kind of solidarity. But we have it.

"Sure, there are guys on the club who don't participate in our chapel services and in our Bible study groups, but I think they look up to those of us who do believe, who do know Jesus Christ as Savior and Lord, because we try to live up to those beliefs. We don't go around collaring the non-believers and badgering them or anything like that. The best way to achieve anything is by example, and that's what we try to do."

That's what Olin and Ora Krause did when they were bringing up young Paul in Flint, Michigan.

"They didn't take me to church and drop me off and pick me

up later," he said. "They took me, and stayed there. We attended the Trinity Missionary Church. I saw from the very beginning what having good, solid Christian parents can mean. I want to show the same kind of example to my children.

"Playing football so many Sundays out of the year, it's impossible to have that kind of continuous family church life. But my wife and I work hard at bringing up our children in a God-centered home. We take them to church with us. It's pretty much the same kind of example we're trying to set with the team."

For more than a dozen years, after an outstanding college career at Iowa, Paul Krause has been playing professional football. He's managed to play without serious injury.

"Lots of careers don't last as long as mine," he admitted, "but I'm fortunate that in all the years I've been playing football, dating back to high school, I think I've missed just one game because of injury. I'm sure God has had something to do with this.

"I'm thankful to the good Lord for the physical abilities he has given me. Without football, I could never have met the wonderful people I have. Without football, I couldn't have traveled as extensively, and it's enabled me to make a good living and provide for my wife and three wonderful children. It's a job, but it's more than that, too. I truly believe it's what God wants me to do.

"A lot of people worry about the future. I don't. If a person is a Christian, God will always show him what to do at critical stages of his life. I'm sure God will have something for me to do when I'm through playing ball. Right now, I can't worry about it. God has used me as a witness in pro football, so that's important to me. I think we have to learn not to question God's wisdom so much. He really does know what's best for all of us."

Volumes have been written about the temptations thrust in the faces of our sports heroes. Access to women and drugs has been widely reported. This was Krause's comment about that: "Sure, those things can be problems in pro sports, but those things can be problems for everyone—for doctors, lawyers, salesmen, you name it. All of us are tempted and there's no point in a Christian saying he doesn't have to deal with temptation. Jesus was tempted. People in the public eye perhaps have more temptations, and another thing, the things they do and say are more closely watched and listened to. We're living in glass houses, you might say. But when the temptation is tougher, the prayers have to be more regular, and more powerful. You really have to pray hard for strength. Now, we all go wrong sometimes, but we have a God to forgive us. If we ask him for guidance and direction through the difficult times, He surely will provide the strength we need."

In the closely-knit society that is professional football, there is close scrutiny among teammates. Player habits are well known to each other. There is no hiding place. Krause sees this as both a challenge and an opportunity: "We're really a family, so it's not a matter of prying into each others' business. It's just that we are together so much that our lives are very open. When a player has something bothering him, it's a pretty safe bet that the word will get around. Maybe some non-believers are looking at Christians and waiting for them to falter, and when we foul up, I'm sure we damage what could be someone else's budding spiritual development. But look at it this way: If other people are looking at you all the time, and you're a believer, and you're successful, and you have a good wife and well-adjusted children, and God has put happiness in your heart, some of that has to rub off.

"As for me, I've been pretty successful. I've played on truly great teams with outstanding athletes. And off the field, I just have to be the luckiest guy in the world. My wife Pam and I have really been together since we were four years old. We grew up together in the same neighborhood. We got married during my sophomore year in college, and we've been blessed with three tremendous children. What more could I ask for? Now, I'd be a real dummy not to think Jesus Christ hasn't had a profound influence on my life, wouldn't I?"

Athletes of all ages have had drummed into them the old adage that says, "And when the Great Scorer comes to write against your name, he writes not that you won or lost, but how you played the game."

Paul Krause is a man who has played on many teams for twenty years. He believes that old adage, but he believes there is much more to it: "I truly believe God wants winners. Sure, he wants us to play the game by the rules, and he wants us to play the game with enthusiasm and with dedication. I'm certain he doesn't punish us if we lose, and he doesn't look down on us in disgust if we've given our best. But I really believe he wants winners, not just in football but in every walk of life.

"It's important for Christians to be winners, to be leaders in school, in business and industry, in the trade unions, in politics, everywhere. The Christian life is one to look up to, to be used as a model of deportment and character for everyone else.

"Yes, I want people to look at Paul Krause and say 'There goes a good football player.' But it's a whole lot more important for them to look at me and say 'There goes a Christian.' If they do that, that means my life has counted for something."

15

No Bad Times

The only thing that has bothered Ken Anderson is that some sports writers and broadcasters keep harping on the point that this outstanding quarterback is the "son of a janitor."

"That really bugs me," said Anderson. "They give the impression I came from a shabby and deprived background or that there wasn't a lot of dignity involved. And that's so far from the truth it's pitiful. It's unreal.

"We weren't wealthy, that's for sure, but we had everything we needed. We had nice clothes and a comfortable home. I'm a lucky individual. I have great parents, and I was brought up in a great atmosphere."

Erik Anderson might have been a star athlete himself, but he was the oldest child in a large family and he never had the opportunity to finish his schooling. It was essential that he quit school and go to work to help support his family. Then his parents died, so Erik and Jean Anderson raised his youngest brother and sister.

"It just disturbs me a little that this keeps cropping up," said Ken. "My father is a proud man and a super guy. He never pushed me. He didn't try to relive his life through his son. But he was always there if I wanted to go out and play catch. If I wanted to hit, he'd throw to me. But never once did he force me to go out and practice.

"I'm sure he never looked at me and thought of any regret he might have had about not getting a chance to play himself. He's the kind of man who'd just be glad I had some ability. He and my mother got their excitement out of watching me play in high school, in college, and now in the pros."

Ken Anderson and his younger sister Barbara grew up in Batavia, Illinois, a small town about forty miles west of Chicago. Life around Batavia was serene and uncomplicated. A young boy could ride his bicycle anywhere in town. There were tennis courts, athletic fields, and a swimming pool nearby. There was basketball in the winter, baseball in the spring, and football in the fall. Ken was good enough to letter in all three of those sports at Batavia High School.

He also was very active in Lutheran church activities—the junior high league, the senior high league—so his life was full and happy. During those days, he did not permit himself to dream about a big-time college or the pros.

"I remember being pretty excited twice during my senior year," he recalled. "I got a letter from the coach of some big school in Arizona. They wanted me to play football. So we sent them some films. Later on, they sent the films back, along with a nice letter explaining they were trying to go for people more in their own area of the country.

"Then I got a letter from Michigan State and they wanted me to fill out this basketball questionnaire that was supposed to be included in the letter. But there was no questionnaire to fill out. So that took care of the Michigan State thing."

Anderson decided to attend Augustana College. It was the logical choice. After all, it's a Lutheran school and lots of young people from Anderson's church and community had gone there.

"It was one of my better decisions," Ken recalled. "I had a super time in college. If I had it all to do over again, I'd do the same thing. I got an excellent education, a good background for life, I made lifelong friends, and I enjoyed every minute of it.

"As for football, we didn't have real good teams. As a matter of fact, there are some high schools in the Cincinnati area that could have given us a tough game. But we played strictly for the fun of it. If it boiled down to missing class or missing practice, you went to class—that was all there was to it. But it was a great experience."

Augustana won only three games in Ken Anderson's final season. More than a few eyebrows were raised when the Cincinnati Bengals announced in the third round of the draft: "Ken Anderson, quarterback, Augustana College."

The Bengals brought Ken Anderson to Cincinnati the next day—while the second phase of the draft was still in progress.

"It was a case of the country boy coming to the city," he recalled. "They took me to a French restaurant. I couldn't even read the menu. A couple of my friends went with me. One is an attorney but he's not my agent. He just went along to look at the contract. I signed the first contract they offered me. The money wasn't what you'd call great, but it was twice as much as I was going to make teaching school. I was pretty nervous at first, but once I got to camp I pretty well knew I was good enough to make the team."

At twenty-seven, Ken Anderson would seem to have the whole world in his hands. For two seasons in a row he has led NFL quarterbacks in efficiency. He is performing for one of the teams of the future in the league, and he is making a lot of money. He's an all-pro selection. He has a beautiful wife and a healthy baby.

"I still have to pinch myself once in a while," he says. "So many good things have happened in my life. My wife and I were talking about it the other night. We just keep waiting for the bubble to burst."

Not unlike a lot of other folks, Ken Anderson relegated God to the second team once he got to college.

"I just sort of put God on the shelf," he said. "I was involved with football and fraternity parties. It seems like I was concentrating on so many other things, I just got my priorities all fouled up. Even though I classified myself as a Christian, I never really made a commitment to anything.

"After I joined the Cincinnati Bengals I met the girl who was to become my wife. She's a Roman Catholic and just meeting her got me started back to church. Then Doc Eshleman came along and I heard him speak at one of our chapel services and it got things back into perspective. That was right before our game against Pittsburgh in 1973. Since then, I've become a Catholic. I still make a lot of mistakes, but I can see a pattern developing in my life and I'm pointed in the right direction."

Ken Anderson says being a Christian helps a player to handle the pressures of the pro game: "Everyone knows there's a lot of pressure in this game, and I think there is special pressure on a quarterback. I know Jesus Christ likes winners, but he likes people who do their best, win or lose. So when I come off the field, if I know I have given my best, I don't feel guilty about anything. To know that I have tried, and given my all, I know is to have pleased God."

Anderson and the Bengals also pleased a lot of fans in 1975. The team went 11–3 and Anderson, for the second year in succession, led the entire National Football League in passing.

Too, Anderson was named the NFL Man of the Year for his citizenship and conduct off the field in helping others less fortunate. But Ken said all that honor did was to make him more aware of his responsibilities and more sensitive to the needs of others.

"About all I did was lend my name to a couple of committees," he explained. "But now the projects are even more meaningful to us. We're on the board of directors for Hope Cottage in Northern Kentucky. It's a place where kids can go for food, clothing, and medical attention. If kids are abandoned, or if their folks simply can't take care of them, they can get temporary housing and lots of help until they can get relocated.

"Also, for three years I've been the honorary chairman for the Easter Seals campaign for the Cincinnati area and I'll do it again this year. It's really fun. And more than that, since Bonnie and I became parents, we've become much more grateful for what we have. We've seen thousands of people less fortunate than us, so we can really count our blessings."

It was suggested to Ken that perhaps his work on these committees is merely God expressing his love, through Anderson.

"Maybe that's it," he said. "It's tough for me to talk about Christianity, really, because I flounder so much. I see the dumb things I do, and I'm so sorry for them.

"But especially since little Matthew came into our lives, Bonnie and I realize more than ever that there are so many things that are more important than football. Both of us realize we are on this earth for such a short time, really. And mostly, we realize we are much more fortunate than most. That's why we feel it is important that we share our time, our talents, and resources. I'm doubly blessed because of the success I've enjoyed in football and the happiness I have in my home.

"Bonnie is a fantastic wife and mother. I really don't know what I'd do without her. We met at a party when I was just about to begin my rookie season with the Bengals, but we didn't start dating until the season began. We became engaged the day after the season ended and got married six months later. She never pushed me to go to church, but I thought it'd be nice to worship together as a family."

The Andersons started to worship at the Church of the Blessed Sacrament in Fort Mitchell, Kentucky. There, Ken became fast friends with Father Grosser, whose brother is the accountant for the Cincinnati football team.

"I got to know him really well," said Ken. "As for becoming a Catholic, it was all my idea. Father Grosser explained things to me, then let me reach the decisions. He married us and baptized our baby.

"Because of my schedule, I couldn't make all the regular classes for instruction, so I'd go over in the mornings and Father Grosser and I would have coffee and digest the sports pages—then we'd start talking religion. It was really easy to relate to him. I used to kid him and tell him if the Catholics had kept Martin Luther happy, we wouldn't have been going through all this business.

"You can go to any church on any Sunday and pick out things you don't like 100 percent. But I love my church life now. I love to be in the same parish every Sunday and worship with the same people. Maybe in some ways I'm still very nondenominational in my thinking, but I think there will be both Lutherans and Catholics in heaven. God is merciful and understanding, and I think all that is required is that we believe in God and believe that his son Jesus Christ died on the cross for our sins and that he will come again. And I believe that!"

16

The Sugar Bear

When we arrived at Lake Forest College on the outskirts of
Chicago to interview Craig Clemons of the Bears, the air was full
of muggy, steaming heat and the newspapers full of ugly, sad
stories.

It was two days before the annual classic between the professional football champions—this time the Pittsburgh Steelers—
and the College All-Stars. It had been a long time since the lowly
Bears had made an appearance in this midsummer game.

The headlines in the newspapers blared forth stories about a
CIA plot to kill Fidel Castro, an ozone alert because of the
polluted air, and a man in California who had unplugged his
kidney machine—choosing death over more agony. "I look forward to a pleasant death, not painful, and not traumatic," the
thirty-six-year-old father of four had said. "I'll go peacefully and
quietly."

The one certainty was that people—Christian and non-
Christian, medical and non-medical—would engage in great and
inconclusive arguments over the moral issue of a man choosing
his own time to die.

"I'm not afraid to die either," the brilliant Chicago Bear defensive halfback had said. "I'd rather live and enjoy life with my
wife and my children. But if I die tonight, it's fine because I
know God will take care of me."

Craig didn't pretend to understand everything about God, nor
always to see and do his will. Over and over, during the course
of our talk, he kept going back to the passages about the Lord
working in mysterious ways his wonders to perform, and the one
from the Book of Romans wherein Paul spoke of all men having
sinned, and coming short of the glory of God.

"I know him pretty well," he explained, "and he knows me
inside out. The Bible says that even the hairs on our heads are
numbered and that a sparrow cannot fall without him knowing it.

So I know he is aware of me all the time.

"I'm aware of him all the time, too, but I don't always perform like I should and I'm sure I disappoint him. But he knows I'm human, that I have weaknesses, and that I'm not as good a man as I should be. But I'm on the right track. And he knows that, too. And most of all, he knows I love him."

Some seasons ago, in preparing a television show about the Detroit Lions, it seemed appropriate to include something about Ed Mooney. Here was a second-string linebacker who never quite made it big in the National Football League, but whose story was more stirring than most any superstar you might name.

Ed Mooney knew that becoming a Christian didn't give him greater physical skills, but it gave him a more secure life, a happier marriage, and peace of mind. He had no difficulty correlating the violent world of professional football with his commitment to Christ.

"I don't think the two are in conflict," he had said. "Sure, football is tough, it's physical, and sometimes it's even violent. But Jesus Christ is tough, physical, and sometimes even violent. I think I was given certain abilities, and I'm required to use them to the fullest. It'd be a sin if I didn't. So I play football."

Craig Clemons has the same philosophy: "There's no doubt about it. Pro football is violent. You can't go around all the time saying, 'Hey, fella, I'm sorry I hit you.' Man, it's a game for hitters. And that's the way I play the game. Sure, there's finesse in the game, but mostly, it's a physical thing. And in a lot of ways it's the survival of the fittest. I'm not saying you have to go around deliberately hurting people and trying to maim them, but it's no game for a sissy. But Jesus was no sissy, and if he were around today—I know he's around but you know what I mean—he'd be a number one draft choice, an all-American and an all-pro the first season."

The mention of the term "sissy" tickled Craig's funny bone. When he first checked into the Bears' camp as a rookie and a number one draft choice—he came with fancy clothes, a luxury car, and a swagger. Two of the Bears' notorious tough guys, Dick Butkus and Doug Buffone, quickly noticed Clemons' mannerisms—Clemons himself describes them as "a little funny walk and an air of sweetness."

"I guess I didn't walk around like some Neanderthal man, and I still don't. If the word 'gay' didn't have such a bad connotation about it, I'd say that's the manner I had—and still do, for that matter."

But the nickname first applied by Butkus and Buffone sticks today, and no one accuses Craig Clemons of being anything but masculine. He thinks that's totally in keeping with his own image of Jesus Christ.

Craig remembers no great conversion, no dramatic transformation from bad to good. Perhaps it's because he was never really that bad and because the church was always an integral part of his life, even as a child.

And despite the fact he was the product of a broken home and never really got to know his mother, and, like Topsy, just sort of grew, Clemons has only pleasant memories of his disrupted childhood.

Craig's mother "took off" when he was four months old, leaving not only the infant but two older children, Carol and LeRoy.

Morris Clemons couldn't hack it all by himself, so Grandma Sarah Clemons and a couple of aunts opened their homes and their hearts. The house was on Bassett Avenue in the south end of Piqua, Ohio. The term "ghetto" wasn't being used then, but that's what it was. There was no telephone, no running water, no indoor plumbing, no fancy stove. As a little tyke, Craig's early chores were to tote water and chop wood for the stove.

Morris Clemons was a laborer, and there was always food to eat and something to wear. Craig did not think of himself as being really underprivileged because there was so much love in the home. The only explanation he got later about the family situation was that there had been "some trouble" and that his mother had gone away. His father was a quiet man.

"The kids were together in the early years," Craig recalled, "but later on my brother moved to Boston with some relatives and my sister got married as a teen-ager. Grandma Clemons was a gentle lady with long, black hair. She was part black and part Indian. She kept me in church and when I started playing football, she told me to say The Lord's Prayer every time I stepped onto the field.

"My dad was a loner and I think of myself as being a loner. He moved uptown when I was going into high school, and I went to live with him. We had pretty good communication even though he didn't talk a whole lot. We didn't do all that much together and he wasn't always passing out a lot of advice. He expected me to be in early on school nights, but I have to say I had a pretty carefree life in those days."

Craig's early church training came at the Park Avenue Baptist Church in Piqua, but by the time he was in junior high school he spent a great deal of time at the Methodist church. The childhood sweetheart he went to the Methodist church to see is now his wife, Theresa, who has given him a son and a daughter.

"When I was playing football in high school, she was my cheerleader, and she stayed on with me through my years at the University of Iowa. I'm lucky to have found a girl who believes as I do, and we're raising our children in the church."

Craig has mostly happy memories of his own childhood, of Grandma Clemons reading the Bible each day, saying her prayers every night, of Aunt Minnie being a strict disciplinarian not at all reluctant to use a switch on mischievous children, of walking to the grocery store with his grandmother, and of carrying water to help with the washing.

The lessons Craig learned as a child have stayed with him, and he tries to use some of the same methods applied twenty years ago but confesses it is most difficult because of our streamlined society.

He remembers the early advice from the Bible, "Train up a child in the way he should go: and when he is old, he will not depart from it" (Prov. 22:6).

"A couple of years ago I was pretty strong on discipline with Stephanie and Jonathan," he said. "You know, when they were at that ridiculous age. I still chastise them, but I'm getting more lenient with them and I appreciate them more. You can't just keep scolding kids all the time because they'll wind up resenting you. I'm convinced it's a lot tougher to raise children now, even though we have more material things. There are so many distractions out there in the world, and so many parents are totally lacking in discipline."

Craig remembers himself as "a pretty good boy" in his teen years and through college. He chuckled when I mentioned the term "backsliding Baptist," something I'd heard for years.

"You know," he said, "I think we're all backsliders in that we stray from the path of good. Not just me and you, but everyone. Only one man ever walked all the way through this world with clean hands.

"I was always aware of God, but it wasn't until I played in the

Senior Bowl in January of 1971 that I came to what I like to call full realization. It was a big game. I knew I had to prove a lot in order to be selected high up in the pro football draft, so I prayed real hard.

"Now, don't get me wrong. I didn't pray to be drafted high or to get a big bonus. But I did pray to God that he would enable me to do my best. As it turned out, I played well enough to be named most valuable player. It meant extra money, and I knew for sure that I had someone else on my side—someone who was invincible."

It is generally agreed that most folks who are believers treat God pretty much like a dose of medicine—to be taken when we are ill. When we are down and out and in trouble, and when all else has failed, we lift up our eyes unto the hills for help. A famous evangelist once said there were more prayers uttered on the beaches of Normandy than at any other place in the history of mankind, simply because there was more fear there on that June day in 1944.

And, like the prescription that takes away our pain, we put God back in the medicine cabinet until we fall ill again.

Craig Clemons wants no part of that. "I know I have to grow every day as a Christian. There's so much I don't understand about his Word and so much that is confusing to me. I have to work twice as hard at studying the Bible as most people. I think you have to work at being a Christian, especially today when there are so many temptations.

"I've strayed, sure. But I was never a wild kid. I've gone out and had good times. I've had too much to drink and I've partied. I could lie, but I know what I've done wrong, other people know, but most importantly, God knows."

The judgment meted out by his peers is the most difficult thing for Craig Clemons to accept in life. "I know I believe in God, and I'm not ashamed to tell people about it—even though I used to be really hesitant about my beliefs—but it's tough when people question me and say things like 'I heard you cuss or I saw you smoke.' Let's put it this way: The Lord and I have an understanding. I know who he is, and I know what he has done for me and what he can do for me. At the same time, I know I don't do as much as I could for him. And that's my hangup."

Craig is reaching for a mature faith, wherein he can endure the slings and arrows. So he reads portions of the Bible that deal with the unbridled tongue, that talk about the suffering we must endure in order to be Christians, and how God is man's only meaningful judge. In so doing, he has become more outspoken even with coaches and the front office personnel of the Chicago Bears.

"Through Jesus Christ I know more about myself," he said. "I'm a more honest person with myself and with others. I have a much greater insight into myself as a football player, but more importantly, as a human being. I treat people fairly. I don't try to hurt anyone."

Craig Clemons used to steal. As a youngster, he rather perfected the art of thievery from Billings' market on Bassett Avenue. "I stole candy, pop, you name it. And I got pretty good at it. But I'll never steal again."

He learned from those early mistakes and feels God made no effort to "get even" with him for them.

"He isn't a punishing God. He's a good God. Now, he does work in strange ways, but I don't think he sits around dreaming up ways to hurt us for the things we've done wrong. The devil tempts us with evil, but God is always holding out good things for us. We're told to have patience and wisdom and stuff like that, and you can only gain wisdom through your mistakes."

Having been a standout running back at Piqua High School, Craig was understandably upset when he was informed at the University of Iowa he'd be switched to a defensive backfield position. After all, the ball carriers get all the glory and most of the money when they turn pro. But an assistant coach, Wayne Fontes, persuaded Craig not to grumble, telling him, "I didn't tell you that you'd be a great running back in college, but if you work hard and apply your talents, you'll be a great pro prospect."

That he was, and now he is an established performer. "But I still have to concentrate and work hard. There are hungry kids coming out every season, trying to take my job from me. I'm being paid to keep some guy from catching passes against my strong safety position, but the receiver often is being paid twice my salary to catch those same passes. You just can't let down. You have to keep concentrating, just like you have to keep concentrating on your faith in Jesus. My talent will be gone some day, but Jesus will always be with me. I live for him, and would gladly die for him—because I know in my heart he died for me and other sinners."

17

The Virtue of Patience

In the National Football League record book, names like Tarkenton, Baugh, Jurgensen, Unitas, Luckman, Tittle, Van Brocklin, and Namath are listed under the heading of "records."

If there was a record for patience, one might find listed the name of Joe Reed. For the most part of a four-season career, Reed has found himself the number three quarterback on teams that employ three quarterbacks. Learning patience was more difficult than learning the plays. He has alternately thought about quitting and pursuing a career outside of the game of professional football or demanding to be traded to a team where he could utilize his considerable skills.

Almost to a man around the league, quarterbacks insist they get too much praise when a team is going well and too much blame when things are not. Reed's problem is that he has gotten little of either. With both the San Francisco 49ers and the Detroit Lions, he pretty much has been a forgotten part of the team.

In the tiny town of Lorenzo, Texas, Joe Reed won all-state honors as the quarterback of a team that won only three games. That enabled him to win a scholarship at Baylor University, but two seasons there proved to be unsatisfactory. He underwent a shoulder operation and coaches decided he could no longer throw the football with adequate efficiency. Being switched to defense didn't satisfy him.

The coach who originally recruited Joe Reed for Baylor had moved on to Mississippi State and he knew of Joe's unhappiness. So Reed transferred to the school at Starkville, Mississippi, and sat out one season in order to become eligible for his final two years of intercollegiate football.

"I feel all of that was a part of God's plan," said Joe. "To get all-star recognition at a little school, to win all-state honors when my team won only three games—well, that just had to be God's plan."

Joe Reed became acquainted with God's plan for him at a tender age. His parents are God-fearing folks who made certain their five children knew the difference between right and wrong. The elder Reed was in the navy for thirteen years, and as a youngster Joe lived in Rhode Island, Guam, Missouri, Oregon, and California. About the time Joe was ready to begin elementary school, Papa Reed figured it'd be better to pack up and head back for Texas where he had been brought up. He'd had a long-standing dream about owning a chicken farm, and raising children with strong love and strong discipline, without the temptations of big city life. So the Reeds settled down in the hamlet of Lorenzo, near Lubbock in West Texas.

"Dad always thought of himself as a failure in some ways," Joe reminisced. "We weren't too successful as chicken farmers and Dad finally gave up and started working in Lubbock. But in reality he's been very successful because he has an entire family that loves him, and every one of the five kids has just about achieved the goals they wanted. To me, that's success."

The Reeds attended the First Baptist Church of Lorenzo. Joe described his early life as happy, disciplined, and moral. He remembers the final service held in the First Baptist Church just before the congregation moved into a new sanctuary: "I was eight years old at the time. My brother Skip—he's about a year and a half older—was sitting with me. We felt we knew Jesus Christ because we had grown up with him. Suddenly Skip went forward and publicly professed his faith in Jesus Christ. I followed him. It was a fairly emotional thing for me. But there was no great and dramatic change in my life. That didn't come until I was twenty-one years old. Then I finally let him start working in my life. That's when I really turned my life over to Christ.

"Sometimes that can be a disadvantage, I think. I mean, growing up with the feeling that you aren't really doing anything wrong or sinful. I was always taught good morals and we had discipline. Anytime I stepped out of line, I felt guilty about it, sure. But when I was saved, I was a very immature Christian. And I stayed immature for a long time until I learned it wasn't enough just to know Jesus Christ. I finally realized that knowing him, knowing what he did for us, isn't enough. The real joy of being a Christian comes from serving the Lord.

"I know lots of Christians who've had much more dramatic turn-arounds than I. I was never in the gutter. I never was much for drinking and carousing. But Jesus Christ saved me from an egotistical life; he saved me from living my life just for me. Now I live for him, and I live because of him.

"And even now I have revival experiences in my own heart. Last year I was speaking in a service. I felt at that time I was leading a pretty good life, and following the Lord, but right while I was singing I got all choked up and couldn't do the song I wanted to do. So I wound up talking all the way through the song. I felt the Lord's spirit within me. It was a spiritual renewal.

"For a long time, I was going nowhere with my faith and I was lackadaisical about my prayer life. I guess I just took it for granted that God was with me all the time as he promised he would be. But I wasn't with him as I should have been. Now, when I go to him in prayer, all I need to do is open his Word. It almost seems like the answers jump out at me. The toughest thing for me to learn has been patience. However, the Bible is filled with answers for those kinds of problems. There are great lessons in the Bible about pain and suffering and affliction. I really enjoy reading Paul's letters—I try to build my life around those things."

It was not always that way. When Joe Reed was embarking on his second year at Mississippi State, he said he felt his life was slipping away from him. There were troubles on the team. He was not playing. He was complaining, blaming the coaches.

"Then I figured it out," he said. "It just wasn't me, that's all. I wasn't the person God wanted me to be. I wasn't happy around people who didn't have high Christian standards. I was trying to be someone else instead of myself. God created me as an individual, and suddenly I decided I didn't have to be anyone but Joe Reed. That's when I turned my life back over to him. So immediately I was a happier person. I was a lot looser on the field. I wasn't unhappy with myself, and so I wasn't unhappy with the world around me, either. And sure enough, things started turning my way. That's the time I met my wife, Stephanie. We got married my last year there, and I was all wrapped up in her, my engineering studies, and football. Since then, I've been able to handle my life pretty well."

Stephanie Josey is a native of Starkville and transferred to Mississippi State from a girls' college.

"She was already a committed Christian and she got me into

the habit of going back to church," says Joe. "Being from a small town, I was reluctant to meet strangers, and I didn't like to go to church by myself. Now, I don't feel that I ever really meet a stranger.

"God has blessed me with a very strong Christian wife, and I can't thank God enough for my family. Our second baby is due before long, and having children has given me even more love for people. Sometimes when I have trouble sleeping, I go into my son's bedroom and look at him curled up between those sheets. I realize then the wonderful miracle God has performed.

"There are a lot of things I cannot comprehend. However, I read the Bible and I'm always trying for more enlightenment. But even Jesus' disciples didn't understand all things. I accept God as the Creator, and I accept Jesus as the Savior who died for my sins and for the sins of all men. That's enough for me."

Joe Reed's first year in the pro football ranks was none too pleasant. He was all the way across the country in San Francisco. "I was pretty lonely. I didn't have that many friends. There didn't seem to be that many Christians on the team, and there wasn't a whole lot of fellowship. One of our coaches was Jim Shofner, now the coach at Texas Christian, and he led our Bible and study group. Stephanie was away from home for the first time in her life. She was sort of homesick and I felt sorry for her, being alone in the apartment a lot of the time."

When Joe returned to the 49ers for his second season, he felt secure enough about his professional future to purchase a home. He and Stephanie also found a church home, the Peninsula Covenant Church. "People ask me about my denomination and I guess I get kinda hung up on that question," he said. "I am non-denominational. I'm just a Christian. That's the way I look at it. And anyone who believes in Jesus Christ as Lord and Master is a Christian. I don't condemn anyone and I don't judge anyone. I try to concentrate on being a Christian.

"Jesus doesn't say you have to be a member of a certain church—or any church at all, for that matter. You just have to believe in him and his saving grace."

Reed figured, after he was traded to the Lions during the 1974 campaign, that he and his family would return to the South to live in the off-season. But he said the Lord has directed the Reeds back to the Redwood City area.

Joe never got settled into a really secure situation in his professional career in San Francisco. He found himself playing first behind John Brodie and Steve Spurrier, then Tom Owen, then Norm Snead.

"I played quite a bit during the exhibition season of my second year there," he said. "Then they didn't even let me suit up for the first three games. I thought about quitting. I knew I could play, and I wanted to be traded somewhere—anywhere at all where I could prove myself, even as a number two quarterback.

"In 1974, I didn't play much at all during the pre-season games. In the last exhibition game Spurrier got hurt and I was thrown into the first league game with really not much practice. Maybe I was looking for excuses, I don't know. I had played some good games and some bad ones. But the truth is, I didn't play very well, and they had every right to trade me. The 49ers did what they thought was best for the team."

Trades are an integral part of any professional sport, and even though some players ask, even demand to be traded, it frequently is a traumatic experience. It was for Reed: "When I got the news, I was told I had to report to Detroit the next day. All my friends were in California. My wife and baby were there. My pastor was there. My neighbors. There really was no time to say goodbye to anybody. I just broke down and cried. Even though I wanted a chance to play somewhere, I had trouble handling it. My little boy was jumping up and down in his crib saying, 'Daddy, daddy, daddy.' He had just learned to say that. It was crushing."

The situation was even worse in Detroit. There, Reed had three quarterbacks—Greg Landry, Bill Munson, and Sam Wyche—ahead of him. So he tried to stay in condition by working out as a running back and wide receiver.

During the 1975 pre-season schedule, Reed got into action for only about one quarter. He went to Coach Rick Forzano and asked to be traded. He would have settled for being cut from the squad in order to try to land a spot on someone else's roster. The Lions refused, and it's a good thing. Wyche was gone, then both Landry and Munson sustained injuries that sidelined them for the season. The job, by default, was Reed's.

His is a quiet, almost boyish Texas shyness. There is nothing flashy or flamboyant about him.

"I just don't think a quarterback has to be a loud guy," said Reed. "There have been a lot of fine quarterbacks who didn't make a lot of noise and get a lot of attention off the field. Frank

Ryan was a pretty studious guy. There's nothing flashy about Johnny Unitas that I recall. Bart Starr, who's a fine Christian gentleman, was pretty quiet when he was quarterbacking the Green Bay Packers to all those championships.

"I just give my best every time I go on the field. The team realizes I'm trying and that I'm smart enough to call a good game and that I can play quarterback. The best way to lead is by example and that's what I try to do. I think I'm proving that I can play the game. I've gained experience. There's always a need for experienced quarterbacks."

Joe Reed hopes, too, someone has a need for a quarterback who's a Christian and who can sing. While at Mississippi State he discovered he possessed a fine singing voice. He loves gospel music and what he describes as country and western music— "although not all the hard country music."

It sounded strange for this soft-spoken young man from the back country of Texas to talk about enjoying performing his songs in public because, in his words, "being a quarterback, I guess I like putting on a show."

"I enjoy all types of music," he explained. "I especially enjoy Mac Davis, Charlie Rich, and Glenn Campbell. I love music that tells a story, and of course, gospel music tells the greatest story of all."

More attention was thrust upon Joe Reed during the 1975 season than at any time during his football career. It is his custom to inject Jesus Christ into every interview.

"Some people have asked me why we don't win every game, if God is on my side," he said. "They figure if God is so great, then he should act in my behalf all the time. But there are strong Christians on other teams, too. And besides, God never promised he'd make life easy for his people. In fact, he told us things would be rough.

"Football gives me a forum and I can reach people I'd never have the opportunity to reach. God opens many avenues for us. Anytime a writer or a broadcaster asks me about anything— about a particular game or play or whatever—I always tell that person about my walk with God. Sometimes they use that part of it. Sometimes they don't. But I have an obligation to tell others about Jesus Christ.

"That's what it's all about. I'm available to do God's work. It's been said many times before, but he knows my capacity. He knows what I can do, and what I can't do. What God is interested in is my availability, my willingness. And I'm saying to him, 'Here am I. Send me.' It's just as simple as that."

It's just about the way a fellow from Lorenzo, Texas, would put it.

18

Raise Up a Child . . .

Judge Williams was the pastor of Pine Grove Baptist Church in Griffin, Georgia. He took great pride in his flock. It was not uncommon for him to castigate his worshipers when he felt they had strayed.

The Judge preached about hell as well as about heaven. His was a fire and brimstone message, and he took particular pains to remind his parishioners about the wages of sin.

His powerful messages had great impact on the congregation, and a particularly strong impact on his grandson, Rayfield Wright. So when Rayfield was a lad of eleven or twelve, he went forward in the Mount Zion Church and dedicated his life to Jesus Christ.

The Reverend Mr. Williams and his wife have played vital roles in the development of their grandson. Rayfield's parents were separated when he was a tyke, so the job of raising up young Rayfield fell partly on his grandparents' shoulders. Even today, when Rayfield makes one of his frequent visits or calls to the old homestead, Grandma Williams is quick to remind him of his Christian responsibilities. With precious little prodding, she will remind him about the sinful old world full of temptation, and call upon her grandson to put spiritual things above material goods.

As a young man, Rayfield Wright sang in the chorus at the Mount Zion Baptist Church.

"In other words," he said, "when the doors of the church were opened, I was inside. That's just the way it was. There wasn't any other alternative. That was the house of the Lord; we were his children and we were supposed to be about his business."

After the death of Rayfield's grandfather in 1950 the family moved to Griffin, Georgia, where his grandmother had attended church before she was married. It was at this time that they transferred their membership to Mount Zion Baptist Church.

In addition to his school activities, boy scouts, and his church life, Rayfield went to work, out of necessity, when he was eleven years old.

"I'm glad now, as I look back on my early life," said Wright. "It wasn't an easy life, I know, but I'm glad I accepted Jesus Christ as my Savior at an early age, and I'm happy that I started to work. It taught me about the real things in life, and it taught me to work hard. It made me want to be something in life. I knew as a child I wanted to make something out of myself."

Had it not been for an understanding recruiting officer, the talent the world of football knows about now might have been lost in the shuffle. Rayfield Wright could never have gone to college without an athletic scholarship. The family simply did not have the money to afford such a luxury. The little change Rayfield made helping a carpenter and working in a wood pulp plant went for necessities. There was no college fund and no thought of attending, even though Rayfield had an outstanding record of achievement at Fairmont High School in Griffin. He was, he felt, more talented at basketball than football.

Several colleges made some scholarship offers, but they were meager opportunities, and besides, Rayfield felt a keen responsibility to help support his two brothers and a sister remaining at home.

He explained how he got to Fort Valley State College, instead of into the United States Air Force: "They had a career day at our high school and the recruiting lieutenant spoke to the assembly about a career in the Air Force. He said that we could go in with a friend on a buddy system and that we'd be together with someone we knew. The opportunity sounded good and the money was all right and I thought there seemed to be a chance to make something out of myself. So a bunch of my friends and I signed up.

"I took the tests and passed the physical and was all set to go. But then, in the early sixties, they didn't seem to be taking in so many guys. So I just waited around, and since my name begins with a W it was a long time coming. They were calling guys in alphabetical order and they just never got to me.

"At that time my cousin was captain of the football team at Fort Valley State and he told the coach about me. I guess he thought I had enough ability to make it so they came to visit me. I'll never forget when he came to Griffin. I explained to him that

I had made a commitment to go to the Air Force and the papers were signed. My family cried because they were so happy I had an opportunity to go to college on a full-time athletic scholarship instead of going into the service.

"But on a Monday morning we all got together and went down to see the recruiting officer who had signed me up. We explained the whole thing to him. I guess he was a pretty good sports fan and I'd have to say he was pretty much interested in community relations, too. Everyone in the town of Griffin knew about my athletic ability, and I think they wanted to see me get the opportunity to go to college. So he said he'd like to see me have that opportunity too. But he told me one thing I couldn't forget—that if I got into any hot water at college, or flunked out for any reason whatsoever—he'd have me in the Air Force. I remembered his words all through college. He's pretty much responsible for me coming out with a B average."

At the age of thirty-one, Rayfield Wright has nine seasons of National Football League experience—and three Super Bowl encounters—to his credit.

"I've had a lot of good things happen to me," he said. "I know a lot of players in the league had childhood dreams of playing pro ball. I never had any dreams at all like that; I just wanted to be successful. Even going to college was out of the question. But as I look back on the good life I've been able to enjoy, I'm just grateful to God for giving me the ability to play, and I thank God that other people noticed that skill and gave me the chance to use it. The success and the achievement mean a lot to me, but every time I talk to my grandmother—and she's eighty-five years old now—she always leaves me with these words: 'Keep the Man in front of you.' And I don't have to ask who 'The Man' is. I know, just like I've always known. And I try always to keep him first in my life.

"She's a strong woman. I mean very strong. She's typical of our family, though. Our roots are in God. I know that's why we're a strong family unit. It's always been that way and it'll continue to be that way because of all the early teachings we got."

Rayfield's Dallas Cowboy team had just lost the 1976 Super Bowl in Miami when the conversation for this book took place. We had talked some years before, in another capacity, when he and the Dallas team were getting ready for another Super Bowl encounter against the Baltimore Colts.

ABC Television News had dispatched producer Bernie Cohen and me to Miami the week prior to the game. Our orders were to come up with an interesting, off-beat but newsy story about some personalities involved in the game. Both coaches had agreed on one point before the game—that the contest would be decided in the trenches. In other words, line play would make the difference.

At that time, Bubba Smith was playing a defensive end position for the Colts and at that stage of his career he was a remarkable performer. It would be Rayfield Wright's job to fend off the charges of big, bad Bubba. That, then, became our story—the confrontation between young Rayfield Wright and the battle-tested Bubba Smith.

Coaches and players had confided in us that some professional football players playing across the line from Bubba Smith had been intimidated by him and might actually be afraid of the combat with him. During an interview, we asked Rayfield, "Are you afraid of Bubba Smith."

Rayfield bared his teeth but it was no toothpaste smile.

"No, I'm not afraid of Bubba Smith. Now why don't you go and talk to Bubba Smith and see if he's afraid of Rayfield Wright."

The Cowboys lost that Super Bowl game on a late field goal, won a Super Bowl game later, then lost in the 1975 encounter with the Pittsburgh Steelers.

It was a Dallas team that was not expected even to be in the Super Bowl. Coach Tom Landry had confided that he felt his young Cowboys were a year or two away from being of championship mettle. Yet, the Cowboys had matured quickly. They had gotten into the playoffs as a wild card team, then got into the Super Bowl showdown by trouncing the Los Angeles Rams. And even though the Pittsburgh team had won the Super Bowl the year before, and apparently had superior personnel, there were those who believed that perhaps this Dallas club was a team of destiny. Early in the game they led the Steelers, only to be victimized by a blocked punt, then a pair of fourth period touchdowns that resulted in a 21–17 Pittsburgh victory. How was it, swallowing that setback after such a stirring season?

"I don't want to come off as a happy loser," said Wright, "because I believe if you're a happy loser, you're gonna be a consistent loser. I'm never happy when we lose. But looking at the whole thing very honestly, I'm very thankful to God, our coaching staff, our teammates, and our fans. I'm just glad we got as far as we did and that we got the opportunity to challenge the Steelers in the Super Bowl.

"Just to participate in football and in a championship game like that makes me get down on my knees in thanks to God. We have to deal with victory and defeat all through our lives from the time we're born. We can't just pile up one victory after another. My faith in Jesus Christ, and knowing he's my strength, enables me to deal effectively with life on every level. In everything I do, I want to do my best, and I want to bring respect to myself, my family, and my team. But most of all, I want to satisfy God. And I believe I satisfy him by giving my best."

One of the most satisfying things to happen to Rayfield Wright was finding the right kind of woman to share his life. Andrea Joyce Wright, he said, fills the bill more than 100 percent: "I'm a lucky man. Andrea and I got married my second year into the pro game. We had gone to college together and dated steadily then. So we knew we were right for each other. She's given me a wonderful family, a son and a daughter, but more importantly, she's given me understanding."

She understands, he says, that pro football players are made to be larger than life and that the hero-worship sometimes gets out of hand. He explains: "Pro football wives have it tough in many ways, and it requires a lot of understanding, especially on the part of the wife. We've been together a long time and she knows me about as well as I know myself. One time, after a game in Texas Stadium, a young lady grabbed me outside our locker room and kissed me on the neck. I guess she was really excited that we won the game. My wife was standing right there, but she didn't get upset. She knows she's number one in my life. In fact, she knows she's the only one."

It gives Rayfield Wright nearly as big a kick to go out and speak to young people as it does to play on the offensive line for the Dallas Cowboys. He feels he can give them a meaningful message.

He came, a poor boy out of the red clay of Georgia, into athletic prominence, and has the things the world generally uses as a measuring stick for success.

"I know kids today are upset with the world, and in a lot of ways they have a right to be," he said. "And there are more distractions and temptations than ever before. I tell the kids that we don't always have control over everything. Sometimes we can't help being poor. Sometimes we can't help some unhappy situations. Sometimes we can't help being sick, and down and out.

"But there comes a time in the life of every man when he can make a decision that controls his destiny forever. A person can turn over his life to Jesus Christ, and whatever his lot may be, he can know that forever and ever, Jesus will take care of him.

"We have to understand that life is a very precious gift. We don't know how much life we have given to us. I believe in a master plan. I believe God has a plan for all of us. If we're not in fellowship with God, it's not his fault. He plans for us to be in fellowship with him. He'd like us to be with him from the start to the finish. If kids could just figure that out—to get on the right track early—they could overcome these temptations and avoid some of the so-called trips they're taking.

"You know, we are all children of God. There's room in God's family for every person on earth. But we have to make the choice, whether to join up and be an active part of that family. He certainly wants us. It's a question of whether we want him. A long time ago, I decided I wanted to spend eternity with Jesus. And that's just the way it is."

19

Nonviolence Is My Game

"I thank God I was brought up in an atmosphere of bigotry and intolerance. I really mean it. I'm grateful I could see it and experience it. Otherwise, I might really be uptight."

Lem Barney is anything but uptight. He's the guy who keeps the Detroit Lions—and everyone else he knows—loose. His teammates and coaches agree they've never met a person with a more happy-go-lucky attitude.

It was not that way in 1974. Lem became a recluse. He withdrew from almost everything and everybody. Even though he played in all but one of the Lions' regular season games, he was not the daring, exciting football player he had been for seven previous seasons. He even shunned old friends. He rarely spoke except to give crisp replies to inquiries.

The massive problems that confronted Lem Barney were dismissed by the media as "personal difficulties." Even though there are those close to this veteran defensive backfield star who know exactly what those problems were, Lem remains reluctant to publicly air those troubles. He will say only this: "A lot of people know I had some troubles, but no one—except me—really knows the inside story. Sometime at a later date, I plan to put it all down, perhaps in a book. But I wouldn't consider telling the full story until after I retire from pro football.

"I really think I have a story to tell, and I think that by telling it I can help a lot of people. But now isn't the time. I know there are lots of rumors, and people have expressed many different opinions about my difficulties, how they began and how I finally handled them. Let's just say it was the most trying year of my life. It was the heaviest cross I've ever had to bear.

"But God pulled me through it all. Without him, I could never have made it. But now it's all behind me. Jesus helped me solve the problems. And because of that, I've made some alterations in my life and have given myself totally to him."

Lem was never really far away from God. As a child in Gulfport, Mississippi, Lem Barney Sr., and his wife, Berdell, saw to it that the Barney children (there were seven of them, but three died in infancy) had a God-oriented life. They grew up in a little Methodist church in Gulfport, and the Barneys provided a living by working as cooks and caterers in hotels and restaurants along the Gulf Coast.

Theirs was a simple, happy life. Lem, the lone surviving son, made sure of that.

"I've never been anything but happy—that is, except for 1974," he said. "I don't know quite how to explain it except that there was a lot of love in our home. I guess I've always figured out ways to be happy. And if the people around me are happy, then I'm happy, too."

In those days, Lem and other members of his family were subjected to racial humiliation. They had to use the public facilities that were designated for use by blacks only. They rode in the back of the buses. They heard all the racial slurs, took their whippings, and turned the other cheek.

"I'm telling you," said Lem, "and I mean it when I say it—it was a great experience. When I was in college at Jackson State, it was a time of turbulence and unrest. Those were the days of the riots, the protest marches, and sit-down strikes. It was all just a part of the experience of growing up. I'm proud that I made it through without any kind of scars, emotional or physical. We knew what was happening. It wasn't a matter of being unaware.

"As a little kid, I knew all about injustice, prejudice, and bigotry. It was just a way of life. We just accepted it as a part of our growing experience. Sure, we felt things always would get better, and they have. They're not perfect, and maybe they never will be. But I can honestly say that I don't have any hatred in my heart. I just don't have room for it. I use the term *brothers* but in reality, all men are my brothers. God made some of us black, others white, and others different colors. But we all have the same God. He's color-blind, and I think every true Christian is color-blind, too. God doesn't have any room in his heart for bitterness, and I don't either. My parents raised me better than that. The toughest times are all behind us, anyway."

More militant blacks at college and in the professional football ranks have urged Barney to become more involved.

"I am involved," he insisted, "and deeply involved. The difference is, I don't want to battle with violence. I battle with love. Those who disagree with me can call me an Uncle Tom or a white man's nigger, but I don't want to do anything to hurt anyone. Names and labels don't bother me. I love everybody. Just because I don't believe in rioting and burning doesn't mean I don't understand the plight of my brothers. I want harmony, and I strive for that. I'm working for a better world for all men, of every color."

Even though he is a veteran of many National Football League seasons and a several-times all-pro selection, Barney retains his youthful enthusiasm not only for the game but for life. That is precisely why his withdrawal in 1974 was so difficult for his friends to take. Just as his cheerfulness had rubbed off on his teammates and friends in seasons past, so did his solemn posture of that one, long season.

Said one of Lem's close friends, Charlie Sanders: "We all knew Lem had a tough cross to bear. All of us would have carried it for him, but he wanted to battle it out alone. Lem just chose to keep things inside him, so we let him alone. But he was aware of our feeling for him and that we'd do anything in the world to help. But in a sense, we all shared his cross."

Coach Rick Forzano talked about Barney's leadership: "Lots of players have great ability—some have great personality—but Lem has a unique blend of the two. When a guy can do the job on the field as well as Lem can—and he's truly a spectacular performer—and then can be the good humor man and a leader in the locker room, you simply cannot measure his value to a team. Lem's back in stride now. Not only his prayers, but the prayers of lots of other people, have been answered and we're grateful."

The Christ of Easter Sunday is the Jesus Lem Barney most remembers as a child in Sunday school: "It's the first thing that really impressed me and stuck with me. I guess I was five or six years old at the time. We had little Easter pageants in our church. I've always liked Christmas, and I understand the meaning of the birth of Christ—but if he didn't experience the cross, if he hadn't been crucified for our sins, and if he hadn't risen from the dead, it'd be tough to convince anyone about eternal life. He beat death. He conquered the grave. He overcame sin. And because of him, we can have life eternal. That's really overpowering!"

As a child growing up in the Methodist church, Lem was

christened. Until the traumatic experience of 1974, he had continued to worship as a Methodist. That year, he joined his wife Martha in the Baptist denomination.

"I was baptized then," he said. "We never really had any differences or problems over church attendance or anything like that. But my troubles made me realize just how much I needed Jesus, so I embraced my wife's particular faith. I had drifted away. I was trying to run things my way. Like lots of folks who turn to him when they get in trouble, I discovered I needed that old fire back inside of me. And like it says in the Good Book, he's always there. He never lets us down. He never turns his back on us. And sure enough, he was right there ready to take me in his arms again and help me. He had never left me."

Lem disdains pious folks who see only the sober, reverent side of Christianity. "Look, the Man intended for us to have fun. I've always thought God had a terrific sense of humor. I mean, He's one guy who really has his stuff together. Sure, I believe in being reverent, and I respect God and his word. But I think he means for us to have recreation in our lives. I'm sure he wants us to laugh and have fun. Look at it this way— what can be more fun than being secure in the knowledge that he died to save us, that he paid the price for all of us? Man, there's a whole lot of joy in that. He gives us tons of reasons to celebrate and be happy. Christians should be happier than people who aren't in the fold . . . a whole lot happier, in fact.

"And the greatest joy is in sharing your faith. I think that's the one thing I've learned to do in recent years. When I first came into professional football, Christians were considered square. But because of guys like Dr. Ira Eshleman, Billy Zeoli, and our chaplain, Lloyd Livingston, everything is out in the open now. We're really out to glorify God. And we're learning about the Bible, and understanding it.

"When I was a kid, I'd read in Genesis and about all I got out of it was a bunch of jibberish about so-and-so begat so-and-so. Let's face it, it was tough for a kid to even begin to understand. And as for the Book of Revelation, all that ever did was confuse me more. I still don't come close to understanding all the things in the Bible and I don't believe there's a person alive who does. But I'll guarantee you this—I understand things a whole lot better than I ever did.

"Christ's message isn't a complicated one. It's really very

simple, in fact. All we have to do is open our hearts and let him in, and he'll take over. But we have to help ourselves by studying the Word. In a lot of areas, through study and through sharing, I've come to a full comprehension of things that used to be mysterious and complex for me. It's almost as if Christ is saying to each of us, 'Here's your ticket. Get on board.' It's almost as if Christ is trying to pay us for the privilege of gaining everlasting life.

"You know, one of the things we sing about in church is that thing called 'blessed assurance,' and Christians really have that. I watch a guy like Billy Graham on television. I see people on his team. I remember the great Dr. Martin Luther King, Jr. You look at people like that and you just know they're on the right track. They glow. They're at peace with themselves because they know God is directing their lives. That just has to be the best feeling in the whole world."

As a youngster in Gulfport, Barney was involved mainly in two things—sports and church work. He excelled in both football and basketball but describes himself as always a tenth of a second too slow to make the relay team in track. He enjoyed singing in choral groups. Once recruited to play football at Jackson State, nearly two-hundred miles from his hometown, Lem immediately leaped to stardom in football. At the same time, he involved himself with Sunday vesper services on campus.

Then, and now in the professional ranks, the elder Barneys kept close tabs on their son to make certain he wasn't getting out of line. His mother taught Lem a long time ago to pray not only at night, but in the morning upon arising, and to this day he begins each day with this prayer she sent him:

> No one knows the power of prayer,
> For someone's always listening there,
> With a heart that hears, and a voice that calls,
> For someone knows when a sparrow falls.

With almost every letter Lem receives from Gulfport he will find a verse or a word of inspiration his mother has clipped from a magazine, newspaper, or religious tract.

"I don't care how strong you think you are as a Christian," Lem Barney advised, "you still have to borrow strength from other people, other sources. Sin is always chipping away at us, so we have to renew our spiritual strength.

"I know I get strength from other Christians, especially guys in football. And our chapel leader, Lloyd Livingston, is a great help to me. He's talked a lot with us about continuing to develop good habits as a Christian. He's convinced me that even though my role is that of husband, father, lover, and provider, I have to do extra things for my family, and put an extra effort into marriage and the home life.

"It's one of those beyond-the-call-of-duty things, you know. You have to put extra effort into your Christian life as well as into a football game. As Christians, we're supposed to grow in love and in knowledge. So we have to put more and more time away for reading the Word or religious books. It's like everything else in life, it's a never-ending learning process. If we want to learn more about God and his teachings, then we have to put more into it.

"Some of the mysteries are still there, but it's amazing how many questions you can clear up in your mind just by searching the Word. Jesus spoke in parables, to be sure, but there's not a whole lot of uncertainty about what he said and what he expects of us. On this thing of racism, I know that God created all men equally. I know God didn't have any prejudice and I'm certain he expects all of his children to have clean hearts with no hatred inside. But let's face it—we're all brought up differently; we're taught in different ways; we're influenced by many things and many people. Sometimes it's tough, but I really do love everybody. I think black is beautiful, but I think white is beautiful, too. Everything God made is beautiful. I believe in my heart that if I can get a man to stop and get to know me and talk with me, I can make him love me as a fellow human being. After all, God is love. And if we love him, we just naturally have to love each other."

20

Super Bowl, Super Empty

The Pittsburgh Steelers had just won their first Super Bowl. Their players were $23,000 richer and the town was delirious. After all, it was the first time in history the Steelers had ever won anything that big.

They were a tough team from a tough town. They were owned by a tough old man, and they won because of a tough defense. The celebration went on for days. Perhaps no town in the long history of the National Football League had been more starved for a winner. Maybe no city appreciated it more. There was nothing blasé about the reception.

One man had an empty feeling about the whole thing. Sure, the money was good and it helped him over some financial difficulty. The championship ring would look nice because it would grace hard-working hands. But for Mel Blount, there wasn't much warmth, there wasn't a whole lot of personal satisfaction in those heroic deeds.

He had started for the world champion Steelers at the right corner-back position. He had played well, even intercepted one of Fran Tarkenton's passes and had helped the Steelers to their 16–6 achievement. But he was not a happy man.

His miseries had dated back to the last Sunday in December of 1974 when the Steelers played the Oakland Raiders for the championship of the American Football Conference. The Steelers had won the game 24–13 and thus earned the right to play the Minnesota Vikings in Super Bowl IX in New Orleans. But in that AFC championship game, the Raiders' Cliff Branch had caught nine passes (a record) for 186 yards and the lone Oakland touchdown. Blount, who had some of the responsibility for covering Branch that day, finally was yanked from the game.

Sportswriters and broadcasters had a field day with that story. Blount was not so upset with head coach Chuck Noll as he was with defensive coordinator Bud Carson. He made no effort to conceal his disappointment and chagrin.

"I felt I was being discredited," said Blount. "I felt I should never have been pulled from the game. It hurt, and it hurt a lot. Then the story was blown far out of proportion. Some writers, I guess, felt I had blown my entire career. Actually, Branch caught only two passes where the responsibility was mine—but writers and broadcasters don't understand pass coverage and lots of other things about professional football. He caught one for a touchdown and another for a good gain—but the press said I was responsible for all nine of his catches."

So while the rest of the Steelers were enjoying the fruits of the Super Bowl conquest, Mel Blount sought refuge at his farm. Every time he feels pressure or gets discouraged or needs to do some deep thinking, he retreats to the land where he grew up at Vidalia, Georgia.

"I grew up there," he said. "It's just a small, southern town with a population of about fifteen thousand. My family—brothers, aunts, uncles, my mother—in all we own about twenty-six hundred acres. It's just a good place to be, that's all."

When Mel was a lad, there were times when he wanted to play or practice his football, but James Blount and his wife Alice had eleven mouths to feed, and there was always work to be done. Oft-times, play and football finished a distant second to the chores.

"Maybe I didn't appreciate the hard work then," said Mel, "but I do now, and I wouldn't trade that for anything in the world. It made me appreciate what I have. I learned about hard work and sacrifice and the importance of a strong, loving family life. I had lots of responsibilities as a kid. I had to feed all the animals, cut the wood, pull corn and take it to the mill. Looking back over my life, I'm proud of all that. It helped make me what I am today. I didn't grow up with everything handed to me."

It was that way in high school, too. There weren't stacks of scholarship offers from the big, major universities in the North.

"In those days, black athletes in my part of the country weren't getting as many opportunities," he explained. "Not every door was opened. I got a chance to go to Southern University in Baton Rouge and I took it. There was some pride involved in that. I was the first athlete in my community to get to go off to a major university."

When he was a junior, he met the woman with whom he wanted to share his life.

"Leslie was a freshman but we knew right away it was the real thing," said Mel. "We got married six months later. She believes in me, and she makes me a stronger person. We've had our share of problems, but we're able to work together to solve them, to accomplish something."

As a child growing up around Vidalia, Georgia, Mel was introduced to Sunday school, church, prayer meetings, youth meetings, and all the rest. "I was pretty dedicated as a youngster, but like a lot of other people, when I got out on my own and left home for college, I started to get away from the early teachings. But once I got into the National Football League, I found the Christian atmosphere again with the chapel services."

Still, Mel said he did not make Jesus Christ the center of his life until after the Super Bowl victory. And on the day he finally turned his life completely over to Jesus, you could say that Mel Blount wore out two horses. This is the way he told the story:

"Winning the championship and the Super Bowl just didn't mean all that much to me. The business of being taken out of the AFC title game and the controversy that followed was just too much to swallow all at once. I really wasn't sure I was going to play any longer. It's not that I had enough money to retire, but I'm not hung up on material things. I feel that as long as a man has control of himself, as long as he has something to believe in and is able to make a living, then that's enough. I don't feel I'll always be able to live the way I do now. Football is just a stepping stone. A person has to prepare himself for the time when it's over. So the issue wasn't money—the issue was whether I really wanted to play any more.

"I felt I had been discredited professionally, and I was at the crossroads of my life. I had just finished my fifth year and was in good shape physically, but I wasn't sure I wanted the game for another minute.

"I love the farm country. I always go there when I get the feeling the world is closing in on me. It's so free and open there. One of the things that really opened up my mind was the fact that I was home again. I'd always felt I had someone I could turn to, someone I could believe in, but I had never really called on the Lord Jesus Christ before and been ready to totally serve him, to really let him come into my life and take the reins.

"Everything was so beautiful at the farm. Normally, I ride my horse for an hour or so, but on this particular day I rode for about four hours. I went back and got another horse. I was doing some hard thinking and praying. I really had a good chance to look at myself. And looking at nature and all of its beauty made me more aware of the power of God. I needed his power, strength, and courage in order to carry on. The longer I was on my horse, the more I prayed and the more the tears kept streaming down my cheeks. That day, I really began to get my life together. That's the day I started having a solid relationship with Jesus Christ.

"When I finally got back to the house, I ran in and told Leslie I had found the answer to my problems. I was feeling better inside and I was happy. I didn't have anything tearing me up. I just felt good all over. I became a brand new person."

The change wasn't temporary. Mel Blount returned to the pro football wars with the Pittsburgh Steelers and when we interviewed him for this book, we were in a hotel room in the French Quarter of New Orleans. A week before, he played a key role in the Pittsburgh Steelers' second straight Super Bowl victory, this time over the Dallas Cowboys. And he had been selected to participate in the Pro Bowl game as an all-pro defensive halfback.

In order to get into the Super Bowl game the Steelers once again had to beat the Oakland Raiders. Once more, Mel Blount had to face Cliff Branch. The second time around Branch caught but one pass, that one coming when the issue had been pretty much decided.

"But you see, none of that stuff really matters," Mel explained. "He's a great receiver, and he'll have great games. I think I can do the job at my position, but I'm gonna get burned sometimes. The real issue is how we face life, how we handle our triumphs and our setbacks, and in the end, where we are going with our lives. The turnaround came for me when I let Jesus Christ take control. I'm convinced that when I became dedicated to him, I, in turn, became more dedicated to the game of football.

"When I came back to camp in the summer of 1975, I had all the strength in the world on my side. I just wanted to come back, take the ability I had received from Jesus, display it, and let the whole world see it. And a lot of people noticed. Even Howard Cosell talked about me all season long. My only goal was to use my ability. You see, I'm a different person mentally, too. It's more than just a physical thing. I have God on my side. I have someone I can depend on. My whole attitude is different. I understand the things of this world much better than I ever did before."

So scintillating was Blount's performance that he made eleven interceptions—tops in the league—and was voted to the Pro Bowl.

"It's an individual honor," he said, "but the glory belongs to God. He's the one who got me here."

Elsewhere in this book there is the story of Terry Bradshaw, the Steeler quarterback, and how he turned his life around through Jesus Christ. Blount believes things like this are a very real part of the success of the Pittsburgh team.

"Every year I see Christian growth on our team," he told me. "Not long ago, Reggie Harrison stood up and gave his testimony, and this year he was the hero of the Super Bowl game against Dallas. I'm not suggesting that God worked any miracles through Reggie. I don't think things happen that way because there are a lot of fine Christian men on the Dallas club. However, having Christians on the team helps us have unity and a spirit of togetherness. We're a family.

"We're all working for the same goal. We're able to talk to each other. Maybe some other teams don't have the togetherness we have, I don't know. But I know we have it. We all try to help each other. And I'm sure that having Christian leadership on the team helps a lot. I know what it's done for me and I've seen what it has done for others."

When Mel Blount goes back to his farm near Vidalia, he stops and talks to the little children. Many of them do the same chores he did when he was their age. They go to the same church, and sing many of the same songs.

Most will never have the opportunity to leave Vidalia. It is unlikely any of them will know the thrill of playing in a Super Bowl. That is why Mel lingers, and answers their questions.

"Sure," he said, "I see myself in them. And I feel that maybe Jesus Christ is using me to show other kids that you don't have to be from New York or Los Angeles or some other big city to make it. And maybe because I made it, some other little kid from some other little dirt-farming town will make it.

"If I can influence those kids to turn their lives over to Christ, and if I can show them what great things he has done for me and what he has meant to me, it'll be better than winning 100 Super Bowl games."

If Mel Blount never plays on another winning football team the rest of his life, he already has taken a position on God's team.

21

God, Family, Football

Perhaps there is no one who can accurately determine how many times in his lengthy career Fred Cox's kicking has decided the outcome of a football game. Maybe no individual on a squad feels more pressure than a kicker. Surely no player is more visible to the fans in a tense situation than the kicker.

Only two players in the long history of the National Football League have kicked more extra points than thirty-seven-year-old Fred Cox of the Minnesota Vikings. Only one has kicked more field goals.

But because of the sensitive area in which he performs and the pressure attached to his job, his successes and failures are more visible to the fans. They are more likely to remember the few he missed than the hundreds he has made.

Cox understands the fans' view of his role. It was a considerable length of time before he understood it himself.

"The toughest thing in the world for a kicker is to put the ones he missed behind him," Cox explained. "I couldn't begin to do that until I got my objectives straightened around. When I came to the realization that Jesus Christ had to be first, my family second, and football third, that's when my life began to have meaning."

Fred and Elayne Cox have four children. They, too, feel the pressure that is on the field goal and extra point kicker.

"When my children go to school," he explained, "they're saddled with the fact that their father is a professional football player. He's on television. He's well-known. If I miss a field goal and the Vikings lose a football game, my children still have to go to school on Monday morning. We all know that kids can be brutal sometimes. Mine get teased by other children, and sometimes it's very difficult for them.

"I realize I'm human, and I don't make all the extra points or all the field goals. But children don't realize that. Sometimes grownups don't accept that, either. But it's a learning experience for my children. It's a lesson in their Christian life, and they need special strength to handle some of those situations.

"My comfort to them is that they are willing to go to school and accept some of the glory when maybe I've made a field goal that brought our team a victory. Therefore, they have to accept the bad times as well. It's not all good and it's not all bad. I tell them that sometimes on the field, or anywhere else in life, you reach out for a bunch of roses and you come up with a handful of thorns. All in all, my children have learned to handle it very well. The Christian teachings they've had are very instrumental in helping them through the tough times."

With football families, fall is a difficult time for family life. The season begins early with six weeks of summer camp, and if you have a good team—as the Vikings generally have—you're playing a lot longer season than most teams.

"Elayne deserves a medal for the extra work she's done," Fred offered. "She's not as fascinated with me being an athlete as some people are. She's very objective about it. She knows I love the game, and she's very understanding. Her strength has really helped me, going back to the time when I rededicated my life to Jesus Christ.

"I had accepted Christ into my life when I was eight years old. I grew up in a Christian home. I went to church every Sunday. I had all the certificates. I knew the right verses of Scripture. But I didn't really understand what it meant to have an active and total commitment. In high school I was totally wrapped up in athletics—football, baseball, soccer. All my objectives had to do with sports. I had no real commitment to a Christian witness. Athletics, not Christ, was first in my life.

"When I got to college, my objective then was to be a professional football player. Once you get there, each year just brings you one step closer to the end of your career. What then? That's when Elayne brought my attention to where my life was going. Or maybe I should say where it was not going.

"It wasn't until I had been in professional football for a couple of seasons that I realized what was missing in my life. That's when I got things in order, and put God first, my family second, and football third. I feel I'm a better football player because of it. And frankly, all the athletes I know that have gotten themselves squared away like this say the same thing— that they're better technically and in every other way because of it."

Fred Cox says a simple prayer before each football game, and in it he asks for his team to do well and for each man on both teams to escape injury.

"I don't pray before I kick, no matter how important the kick may be," he added. "Other guys on the other team have needs, too. The Scripture says everything works out for good. I assume the kicks that are blocked . . . well, maybe the other guy needed it more. I really don't know. Of course, I want to make every one. I want to kick the ball out of the end zone every time I kick off. But it just doesn't work out that way. It's part of a Christian's understanding to accept whatever comes along."

Each time Fred Cox talks about understanding, his conversation goes back to his wife. He calls her job "burdensome."

"A lot of the time she has to be both mother and father," he explained. "I work four days at my chiropractic clinic, so I'm on the go a lot. We are heavily involved with our church. Football takes up a lot of time, it seems, almost the whole year round. I'm convinced an athlete really needs a strong wife to answer all the demands of a growing family. There's a terrific amount of pressure on everyone, but Elayne is just beautiful about it."

As he spoke, it was only ten days until Christmas Day 1975. Fred Cox and the other Vikings had every intention of being busy with football until the latter part of January. On Christmas Day, they would be in Tulsa, practicing for the NFL play-offs. Elayne and the four children would pretty much plan Christmas on their own and arrange to be with the grandparents on Christmas Day.

There are many other demands on Cox and people don't always understand that he cannot fill every request. "That's one of the toughest things to make people understand," he admitted. "I have football, and I have a business. But more than that, I have my family. Naturally, when people know you are a willing witness for Christ, they want you to speak and make appearances. And I do a lot of that. And it's difficult to say no. But sometimes it cannot be helped.

"But overall, most people comprehend my situation. They know, as I do, that football doesn't last forever. I'm trying to prepare myself to take care of my obligations after football is all over."

Another thing that sometimes bothers Fred Cox is that he does not have all the answers about faith: "It happens in my outside business and it happens in football. People will come into my office, knowing I'm a Christian—or younger players will come to me—and they seem to think that because I've been around a while that I must have answers they don't have: I don't profess to be what you might call a 'professional Christian.' By that, I mean I'm not qualified to give a lot of advice on every level.

"But being a Christian gives me a certain advantage over the non-Christian, I'm sure of that. But it's that way in every walk of life. A Christian has problems like the non-Christian. The difference is, the Christian can find the solutions and answers. He can read the Scripture and find his comfort and peace. And the Christian knows why lots of things are happening, but mainly, he knows what he's doing with his life and where he's going. The young Christians—I call them baby Christians— have to grow gradually. They have to experience all the ups and downs and come to grips with their problems. It doesn't happen overnight with anyone. But if we're maturing in our faith, we're much better equipped to handle life's problems no matter how overwhelming they may seem at the time."

Pro football players agree that there are more professing Christians in the game today and that athletes are much more willing, even eager, to speak aloud about their faith. Cox thinks that may be because of the violent nature of the game and the image so frequently presented of the professional football player. He said: "Pro football players are very much aware that they're frequently painted as animal-types. Most people think of pro football players as barroom brawlers, very combative people. It is a violent game, pro football. But today's player isn't out partying all the time. That's as far from the truth as anything could be. Maybe that's why the Christian athlete is speaking out so readily today. It's up to us to change the image of the pro athlete."

Until about 1968, open Christian activity on the Minnesota Vikings' squad was limited. When chapel services were started, only four or five players would attend. The Christian athlete was the exception, not the rule.

"I've involved myself with several good organizations," Cox said, "including the Fellowship of Christian Athletes. Over the years, some coaches who didn't even profess to be Christians have strongly urged their players to attend religious summer conferences. They've seen some great things come out of those sessions. Maybe they couldn't even discern what it was—but whatever it was, it made for better human beings and thus more successful football teams.

"We've all gained a lot of strength through these activities. When one life is changed, that's the greatest testimony of all to inspire someone else to change, too."

Many of the pro football players work with young people. They've explained dramatic conversions through speeches and the media. As a result, there's much more Christian activity at the junior high and high school level. But Cox feels he's more successful as a witness to the older crowd.

"Let's face it, I'm thirty-seven years old," he explained. "I love kids and I've spoken to a lot of young peoples' groups. But I find I am more effective in dealing with people in their twenties and thirties. Perhaps they identify more with me because of my age and because I have four children.

"I believe that if you save a young person, you have to work backwards through the parents and sometimes that can cause turmoil in the home. If a child in a non-Christian home finds Jesus, there can be squabbling. I find it's a lot easier to work with parents. I've seen it right in my own neighborhood, where parents made a commitment to Christ and thus changed their entire family life.

"Believe me, that's a wonderful thing to see. And there's no turmoil. Parents still have tremendous influence over children, no matter what kind of troublesome society we hear and read about. Parents are still in command, or at least they're supposed to be. And when you save a parent, more than likely you've saved a family."

22

Wanted: One More Trophy

He came into professional football with the Heisman Trophy in his arms, tons of good publicity in his scrapbooks, and a future secured by the comfort of a lucrative contract.

He had the reputation of a solid, dependable, and durable performer who in three seasons of varsity football at Oklahoma had never had a serious injury. He was confident he could perform with the professionals.

But would he be accepted by his teammates? That was the question that burned down deep inside him. After all, he was a hick kid from a hamlet in Oklahoma who had had hundreds of glittering trophies and awards thrust upon him and who now would be stopping off in the big cities like New York, Los Angeles, and Chicago.

Steve Owens really had never been away from home. Sure, he had gone from his birthplace of Gore, Oklahoma, to Miami, Oklahoma, when he was a little child but even that had been upsetting for him. And he had gone from Miami to Norman, Oklahoma, to play college football, but that was almost like not ever leaving home. He had made trips with the football team, and he had gone to The Big Apple to accept the Heisman Trophy given each year to the young man voted the finest college football player in the land. But now he would be pulling up roots and putting down new ones. And he was more concerned about being accepted than about whether he could cut the mustard with the pros.

Perhaps he was not emotionally prepared for the hazing a rookie gets. Maybe he could not totally comprehend the hard kidding he'd have to absorb for having won the Heisman Trophy and for getting a fat contract. Steve Owens says he's still paying dues for that: "When I came here, I was really naïve. I guess I was pretty country. I didn't exactly know the proper way to do things. Anytime a person goes to a new environment there's a certain anxiety, and you have to sort of feel your way along. But I wasn't prepared for anything. The Detroit Lions had always had the reputation for being tough on the field and pretty wild off it.

"The number one thing a rookie wants is to be accepted in any way he can. But what I didn't realize—and it took me a while to catch on—is that there's just one way a football player can ever be accepted, and that's by performing on the field.

"I had things crossed up in my mind. I didn't worry much about my performance on the field. I felt that would take care of itself. I wanted to be accepted as a person. I wanted to go along with the guys and have a good time. Just to be asked was important. It was tough all the way around for my first two years. It was difficult for my wife. I went to the team parties and stayed out late. It was totally disrupting to my homelife.

"But Barbara was a lot more mature than I was. She really understood what was taking place. And it was Barbara who finally brought me to my senses and made me realize what was happening. I wasn't putting anything over on her at all.

"One day it all came together. It occurred to me that the only way I could ever totally be a part of the team was through my performance. If I didn't do the job on the field, I could never be a part of the club. Following someone else, going along with every suggestion for a party, wasn't me at all. I was trying to be someone else. I just got smart and decided to go back to being Steve Owens."

The most embarrassing moment of Steve Owens' life came one morning when he checked into the locker room for practice. As with many of his teammates, he didn't feel like working out. It had been a late night for them. It had been party time, and Steve was among those partying.

The magazine published by the Fellowship of Christian Athletes had already been circulated around the locker room by the time Steve Owens arrived. His picture was on the cover, and inside was the story of Steve's Christian commitment.

"It was embarrassing for me," he recalled. "You can't believe the amount of harassment I got. It went on for days and weeks. People just don't let you forget something like that. But I had it coming—sick as I felt about it—I had no defense. I was being a hypocrite. I knew it, and my teammates all knew it, too. I guess that's the day I started to think about my relationship with God—how inadequate I was—and how I was short-changing him, my family, and myself."

Today, Steve has changed his priorities. "I'm a much stronger Christian now than I was before," he explained. "I'm still not the Christian I want to be and that I can be. But I'm moving forward. I believe my relationship with God has only scratched the surface, but I have my goals now. Like Paul said, we strive for that high calling. He didn't say we ever reached it, but all God asks is that we work toward it. And now I'm doing that. Now, I know I am on the road going up. Sometimes I slip, but I pick myself up right away and get back on the track."

The 1975 football season was a wipeout for Owens. He had suffered a serious knee injury in a game on Thanksgiving Day 1974, and the knee was slow in responding to treatment. It was still not strong when he reported to camp in midsummer, and there was speculation his brief professional career might be over. By the time he got to the point where he might have helped the Detroit club, the season was nearing its conclusion, and it was decided to hold him out of action for the rest of the year to avoid the risk of further injury.

"It was the smart thing to do," said Owens, "although it was a tremendously hard thing for me to accept at the time. I wanted to play, and I knew I could play and contribute to the team. Sitting around is the worst part of the game."

It is even more difficult when you're accustomed to being a workhorse. During his college career a typical Steve Owens' day would be to carry the football thirty times. And in the final game of his collegiate career, against Oklahoma State, he carried the ball fifty-five times. Oklahoma won the game 28–27, and Steve remembers it as "the only time in my life I ever called time out. I was really bushed. Chuck Fairbanks was the head coach, but Barry Switzer, who's now the head coach, was then the backfield coach. He called down from the press box and told me not to call any more time outs. He laughed and said I could have plenty of rest after the game. They were great coaches and had a wonderful influence on my life."

Even though he was recruited by more than sixty colleges and universities, it never occurred to young Steve Owens to go to college anywhere except at the University of Oklahoma.

And it was at the University of Oklahoma that Steve Owens came to know Jesus Christ. He told this story about growing up in Oklahoma: "I was born in Gore, Oklahoma. It's a little town of about five hundred people. My dad was a truck driver, and he was gone a lot. We kid him about that—he must have been home pretty often because he and Mom brought eleven kids into the world. Nine of us are still living. I had a brother and a sister who died very young.

"Mom was pretty religious as I was growing up. My family was mostly Pentecostal but now they're Lutheran. All of us were taught to believe in God. My dad was a good and moral man, but he wasn't quite so caught up with Christianity as my mom. He was tough—a strong disciplinarian. We'd get by with things when he was on the road driving, but we'd catch it when he got home. But fifteen minutes later he'd come around and squeeze us and give us a dollar or two.

"Honestly, I don't remember much about life in Gore, but I remember moving to Miami, Oklahoma, a town of about 14,000 people, when I was in the first grade. I recall being very frightened. It seemed like the other end of the world.

"The thing I remember most is something I asked Mom when we were on the road to our new house. I was as curious as any six-year-old, and I asked her how many eyes God had. She told me he had two, just like we did. So I wanted to know, then, 'If he has only two eyes, how can he watch over everybody in the world?' She told me God could do anything and everything. At that age, I just accepted what she told me.

"You know, I'm so proud of my background. We didn't have much, but my folks worked hard. My father had a tough life, making a living driving thousands of miles every week of his life and being away from his family. And Mom had to work hard to take care of all of us. She picked cotton when she was eight months pregnant.

"Maybe that's why I'm so thankful for what football has given me in terms of security. When we moved from Gore to Miami, we sold our house and land and everything for two-hundred-fifty dollars—so you know it wasn't much. Moving from there was just a better opportunity for Dad, even though it mean spending more time away from his family."

It is a great curiosity that Olin Owens never saw his son play a single high school football game. And from the time Steve began his high school career it was apparent he'd be a star. As a senior, he and Rick Baldridge were selected as the co-players of the year in Oklahoma. Both were fullbacks, and both wound up at Oklahoma as roommates. As it turned out,

Baldridge had a profound influence on the life of Steve Owens.

Olin Owens thought of football as something between a game and a waste of time. Much of the time while Steve was playing, he was working. But even when he was home on a Friday night, he did not attend the games. Olin was content to read about Steve's exploits in the newspaper. Not once did he compliment Steve on his deeds. He assumed that when his son was all through with his high school games—football, basketball, and track—he'd get a decent job like everybody else. College was out of the question. The Owens' budget surely did not include college.

The Owens family, seven boys and two girls, lived on a truck route. A coin laundry was next door. Across the street was a beer warehouse. "There were ten of us in all, since my grandmother lived with us," said Steve. "We had just a little three-bedroom house. When people ask me where we all slept, I tell them we slept wherever we could find a spot to lie down. But I don't have a single unpleasant memory about my young years. Miami is a model town, just perfect for a kid to grow up in. The people are friendly and civic minded, and there are great programs for the kids.

"My mother took special care of us. She's what you might call a 'clinger.' When she gave birth to her children, she figured they were hers for life. It was a real traumatic experience for her when the kids grew up and left home. She had trouble handling that.

"There was love, but there was also discipline in the home. My brothers and I used to fight all the time, and since I'm the biggest in the family, I would take on two at a time. I remember one night we were making a lot of racket, and Dad was trying to get some sleep because he had to go to work early in the morning. When he roared into the bedroom, I slipped out the door and ran outside. He ran out after me—he didn't have any shoes on—and cut his foot on a piece of glass.

"I was scared to stay out and scared to come back into the house. It seemed like I stayed out for hours, but I'm sure it wasn't that long. When I finally got in, he gave me a going over with that thick belt he wore. Forget all that family democracy stuff. In our house, it was a dictatorship!"

Jim McKenzie was coaching at Oklahoma when Steve was completing his senior year in high school. He, and other coaches, began streaming into the Owens' household to recruit Steve. It was then that Olin Owens realized that football could be more than a game for his son.

"He really got taken with the whole idea then," Steve recalled with amusement. "It was funny, in a way. He hadn't said a word about football up to that time, and all of a sudden he and Mom were sitting around talking to twenty or thirty different coaches from all over the country."

Involved as he got—and once Steve began his college career the entire Owens family would drive to Norman for the games— Olin Owens never once tried to direct Steve's career nor make his decisions for him.

One decision could have been particularly tough. A major university offered Steve Owens nearly as much money—in cash, under the table—as his father made for driving a truck for an entire year. Steve explained: "I got offers of money from a lot of schools, and as long as schools are competing for talent, there'll always be cheating. I was a little naïve when it all began, but you learn quickly. And let's face it, some players can be bought. When I was being recruited, I was offered lots of different things—cars, clothing allowances, free fraternity dues. I visited one particular school, and I don't know whether they thought I was lukewarm or not, but they asked me to come back for a second visit. When I did, they laid it right on the line—offering me all the usual things like a car and clothes. But then they offered me five-thousand dollars in cold, hard cash. I'll admit it was tempting.

"I went home and sat down with my parents and explained the whole thing to them. I asked them what they thought. I'll never forget what my dad told me. He said 'Son, I want you to do what you really want to do. We're not going to get involved in where you want to go to college and play football. But I'd hate for you to go somewhere and have to feel like you were a bought player.'

"Right away I knew what I was going to do. The only school I really wanted to attend was the University of Oklahoma. If I had gone out of state, I'd have felt I was betraying everyone in Oklahoma. And I guess they'd have thought that way, too. It was just a matter of loyalty and allegiance, and I've been rewarded a million times for that decision."

But Steve's freshman year at Oklahoma was a rugged one, physically and spiritually. "I had pretty much gotten away from religion. As a kid, I had the early experience with the Assembly of God Church. Then my family became involved with the Mount Olive Lutheran Church in Miami, and I was baptized when I was in the eighth grade. It was more of a ritual than anything else, though. Mostly, I remember going to classes to prepare for it. But I didn't have any real emotional experience with Jesus Christ.

"When I got to Oklahoma, I got hurt right away. Some ankle sprains are worse than broken bones, and this one was. I was in a cast for a long time, and since I'd never been hurt before, I just didn't know how to handle that type of setback. So I quit going to classes. I told Rick Baldridge, my roommate, that I was going to quit school and go back to Miami and get a job. It was the first time in my life that everything didn't go well.

"Everything had been perfect up to that time, but now I was with a lot of other good football players. I was just one of many, and down deep everybody likes to be the star. I was just coasting, getting by with as little effort as possible. Then I had this long talk with Rick. Even though we were both competing for the fullback slot, we were good friends, and he encouraged me all the time. I finally played in the last two freshman games and did well. Unfortunately, Rick had knee surgery his freshman year and didn't come back as well as he might have.

"And through it all, he was much more gracious than I would have been. You just couldn't find a better human being than Rick. A man just has to find out what is most important in his life—whether it's football or money or whatever. With Rick, it was Christ then and now. When he shared that testimony with me, I understood what made him tick. He really had his priorities in line. I envied him. He lived a God-centered life day in and day out, and more than anyone else it was Rick Baldridge who got Steve Owens on the right track. It was then that I truly accepted Jesus as my Lord and Savior.

"I'll always be grateful to Rick for his great influence on my life. I'm human and still make a lot of mistakes, but I'll tell you this—when I sin, I feel guilty about it. And a chaplain told me that's encouraging, because if you sin and don't feel terrible about it, you are in a heap of trouble with your spiritual life."

Steve's college career was studded with success. He won a starting berth as a sophomore fullback and led the Big Eight in rushing. Each year he got better.

His professional career has been marred by a series of injuries. As the Lions' number one draft choice in 1970, he suffered a shoulder separation and missed more than half the season.

Happily, Steve was entirely healthy in 1971 and rushed for more than one thousand yards. He thought the injury bug was behind him. Then the following year there were broken ribs and a pulled hamstring. Muscle injuries slowed Owens in 1973. Then came the crippling injury in 1974.

During the long months of rehabilitation, Steve was tempted more than once to quit the game. His wife, the former Barbara Stoner, encouraged him to quit, rather than risk permanent injury.

"But I can't quit now," he insisted. "I don't think I could live with myself unless I prove that I can still perform well. I'm a firm believer in Romans 8:28—that all things work together for good if we believe in God. I know in my heart that God has a plan for me, and he plans for me to play football again, otherwise he wouldn't give me the strength to endure this injury.

"Maybe this is all part of his plan to test me, I don't know. But if it's a test, I'm up to it. I'm in great shape and will play well in 1975. I'm certain of it. I love the competition, but the thing I love most is feeling sore all over after the games. That's a sign you've worked hard and given of yourself for the good of the team."

Steve believes pro football is changing. Teams are more disciplined. Players are better behaved, despite occasional reports of drugs and wild parties. There aren't so many cliques.

"Guys are freer with each other now," he explained. "Maybe the young guys coming out of college are more aware, I don't know. Our guys on the Lions are very close-knit, but everybody does his own thing. When we have a team get-together, everybody shows up. But if a guy can't make it for one reason or another, that doesn't make him an outcast. There's not the pressure for acceptance that I felt when I started.

"The temptations are the same—maybe even greater because of the so-called open society in which we live. There's always the opportunity to foul up. But it seems to me we're getting stronger, morally, in some ways. I know more and more of our young players have a strong commitment to God. And I'm sure that makes for more unity on the team. We draw strength from each other.

"Not every guy believes the same way or has the same

philosophy. We all may apply our beliefs differently. As for me, I know God is Someone I can always talk to. He'll always listen to me. I have lots of faults, and I'm not a perfect example of what a Christian should be. But I know he's a forgiving God, and he not only sees my faults, but he understands them and forgives me for them. I may con you and my teammates, but I can't fool God. He knows what I'm going to say even before I say it. He knows my every thought.

"This is the first time I've ever really opened up and talked squarely about myself and God. I guess it's just time to bring everything out and put it on the table. God already knows about it, so we might as well tell the world."

Steve Owens has one strong dislike. He does not like to be called "former Heisman Trophy winner Steve Owens." That's because, he says, that award was for something he did a long time ago. The trophy he seeks now will never tarnish.

23

Just You and I, Lord

Life on earth has been described as a succession of ups and downs, a series of peaks and valleys—a compromise at best.

Mark Moseley is twenty-eight, and surely he will have successes and reversals later on in life. It is doubtful, though, if he will sink any lower than he did in the early 1970's.

Consider that he had enjoyed a spectacular high school and college athletic career. He was—in his words—"a pretty big deal on campus."

He had been drafted by professional football and performed successfully in the pro ranks. For reasons that he still cannot understand, he was released. His first marriage had failed. He had said his painful goodbyes to a pair of darling little girls.

Suddenly, every door in the National Football League was slammed in his face. He scuffled for a living to support his two children and a new bride. Just when he thought he had hooked on with one club, he flunked the physical examination. Doctors told him he had a ruptured disc and that he would never kick again.

For two painfully long football seasons Mark Moseley sat in Texas and waited for the telephone calls that never came. His letters to twenty-six National Football League teams went unanswered. His telephone calls were not returned.

"Everything I had held dear was ruined. The divorce and leaving behind two precious kids was a terrible ordeal. The career that I thought I had in the palm of my hand just evaporated. I had drifted away from God and his teachings.

"I kept kicking every day, hoping to find a way to get back into football. I knew I could do the job, but it seemed no one even wanted to talk with me. I'm sure everyone else had given up on me, and it's no wonder. One day it occurred to me how empty and meaningless my life really was. I hadn't paid any attention to my early teachings. I had been a participant in church, but I really wasn't a dedicated, committed Christian. I had "gone forward" in church when I was eight years old, but I don't even remember anything about that.

"My home life had been good. My folks are great Christians. Being in church was the normal thing to do. But until all those setbacks, I had not really turned my life over to Jesus Christ. I had not made him the King of my life. I was on the throne, and he was somewhere in the circle around the throne. In the midst of my despair I sat down and had a long talk with my wife about it. We had a pretty good marriage up to that point. But we had our difficulties. I'm not saying the marriage was in trouble, but it wasn't the fulfilling relationship that it was later to become. In every part of my life, something was missing. And it wasn't hard to figure out—that something was Jesus Christ."

The 1972 and 1973 seasons were total wipeouts for Mark Moseley. But then it all changed in 1974 as he found himself kicking field goals and extra points for one of the NFL's finest teams, the Washington Redskins. Personnel Director Tim Temerario responded to a letter Moseley had written two years earlier and invited him to come to training camp. He not only won the job, but wound up the sixth leading scorer in the league. And he retained the job through last season.

"My father has always been a tremendous supporter for me," said Mark, "and I think even he was about ready to give up. I'm not sure that my wife hadn't given up, too. And then one day I just thought about all the disappointments and I said 'It's just you and me, Lord. No one else can help me but you.' And I really believe he did help me and that he continues to help me. He gave me the courage to face that adversity, and I know in my heart if I hadn't gotten another opportunity to play, he'd have given me the strength to accept that, too."

Mark Moseley had to face few adversities in his early life. He grew up in a Southern Baptist church in Wyoming where his father, Jack, was a professor at the University of Wyoming. Jack and Rossie Moseley centered their life around the church. Looking back, Mark feels he went forward in church perhaps because it was expected of him.

"I don't want to call it pressure," he said, "but I think in those days it was commonplace for a youngster to make a public profession of faith at about that age. Maybe with some folks it still is, but with my own children I think the parents' obligation is to provide the right atmosphere, the proper Christian teachings, then let the children decide for themselves when they want to turn their lives over to Jesus Christ.

"On the other hand, I miss some of the things people used to do in church—things we seem to have pretty much gotten away from in these modern times. I always enjoyed the potluck dinners and ice cream socials in the church basement. Matter of fact, I think it'd do folks a lot of good to get back to that sort of thing. I remember having great times at church. It was a real togetherness sort of thing, and everybody was involved in a total church life. The problem, as I learned later, is that while I was involved with the church, I was not really involved with Jesus Christ. I had to have my socks knocked off before I finally woke up and got down on my knees and asked God to forgive me, to straighten out my life and make me a better person."

There were no complexities in the life Mark Moseley knew as he grew up around Livingston, Texas. His was a happy family. Athletic competition occupied much of his time and nearly all his energies. He lettered in football, basketball, track, and baseball, winning all-state honors in three sports.

"I don't think I was really cocky about it, but my wife says I was," Mark laughed. "But remember, she was from another town, and we played her school every year and nearly always beat them."

Victories came one after another. Life was simple and happy. Mark got better than average grades. He was sought by many colleges and universities. He chose Texas A & M but lasted just one semester.

Gene Stallings was the tough taskmaster at A & M, and Moseley never took to Stallings nor to his methods. "It was just a personality clash, I guess. He's a good man. It was his job to turn the football program around there, but in my opinion he went about it a little too strongly. I was enthusiastic when he and Jack Pardee recruited me for Texas A & M, but it wasn't long before I was ready to give up football for good. I had a bad taste of it, for the first time. It just wasn't fun, and I saw no reason to continue. So after one semester I transferred to Stephen F. Austin College."

The new college was closer to home—only sixty miles away not only from home but from Mark's girl friend, Dalva Rowe. He and Dalva got married just as Mark began his new semester.

Within a year they had a baby girl. A couple of years later they had another. Marriage was satisfactory, college was okay, and football was tremendous. He played quarterback for two seasons until he got a banged-up knee. In his senior season Mark concentrated on kicking field goals and extra points. It was the thing that was to give him his most satisfying and most heartbreaking moments later in his professional career.

When the pro football draft took place after Moseley's senior year, he was not among the top selections. Even though he was no higher than the fourteenth round choice of the Philadelphia Eagles, he felt confident about a career in the professional ranks.

"It's funny," he recalled, "but when I was picked, I was fairly confident. I was a green kid who'd never been any more than sixty miles away from home—except an occasional weekend trip when I was being recruited just out of high school—and here I was heading for Reading, Pennsylvania, and a pro football camp. And when I packed my gear, back in 1970, I packed figuring I was going to stay. We had about ten or twelve kickers in camp, but I kept surviving one squad cut after another. Finally it boiled down to Sam Baker and me. Then he was cut, and I was the kicker for the Philadelphia Eagles."

Dalva did not accompany Mark to the north country. She was back home in Texas, expecting their second baby.

"Our marriage just wasn't working," said Mark. "We were awfully young and very immature when we got married. We just weren't ready for those kinds of responsibilities. We were at each others' throats constantly. I guess we just drifted apart. By the time I was through with my rookie year, we agreed that a divorce was the only solution. It was heartbreaking, believe me, leaving Michelle and our new baby, Ellen, behind. She was only a few months old when it happened. When the thing finally ended, it was a terrible shock. Divorce was unheard of in my kind of life, and here I was in the middle of one. And the hurt goes on, because of the children."

Mark Moseley's faith was as shaky as his marriage had been. There was a lot of drift and no direction. Only his football career seemed satisfactory.

Mark kicked fourteen field goals in twenty-five attempts in his first season, not bad for a rookie performer. Late in that campaign, though, he hurt his hip. It was uncertain whether he'd fully recover, so the Eagles drafted another kicker after that season. When Mark checked back into camp, he had to battle Happy Feller of Texas for the kicking job. On the final squad cut Moseley got the bad news. The Eagles decided to keep Feller.

With the start of the regular season just around the corner, Moseley had acquired a new wife and lost a $15,000-a-year job. What appeared to be such an exciting, fresh start toward a new and prosperous life suffered a major blow. But Sharon Irene Allison Moseley had an abundance of confidence in her new husband.

They had dated briefly when Mark was at Livingston High School and Sharon was at Woodville High, some thirty miles away. But they had not seen each other since, until Mark decided to call her one evening.

"I was sitting around home doing nothing," he recalled, "and I thought about her. So I called her. Three weeks later we were married. We knew the problems we had to face, and we knew about the uncertainties of professional football, but we felt we were both mature enough to handle them. And we have been, but only because we put God into our lives and into our home.

"When I was cut by the Eagles, Sharon and I had no money— nothing. We had a car, and everything we owned in the world was in that car. We hit the road for home and decided to stop by New Orleans on the way to Texas in the hope the Saints would take a look at me. But they weren't interested. I called lots of teams but nothing happened. Finally, I went to Houston and camped on the Oilers' front door. I almost forced them to take a look at me, I was so determined to make it. After about three days they signed me, and I spent the 1971 season with them.

"I led the league in percentage kicking that year and had no reason to believe things weren't working out really well. Ed Hughes was coaching the Oilers, but he left and Bill Petersen came in the following year. After two games, he released me. I was out in the cold again. Even though it was the second time I'd been cut, I just knew I'd get with another club."

But he didn't. Not that day. Not that week. Not the next week nor any week for the rest of the 1972 season. He scratched out a living running between Houston and Livingston, working heavy equipment for his father. The following season, the Oilers' new general manager, Sid Gillman, called and suggested Moseley come in and sign a new contract. He did, but doctors refused to pass him on his physical examination because of a ruptured disc. Moseley was at the bottom of his emotional ladder as he headed back home. The only footballs he kicked were those Sharon held for him.

Then, out of the blue, came the phone call from the Redskins—and Moseley launched his career all over again with the beginning of the 1974 campaign.

Being with the Washington Redskins strengthened Mark Moseley spiritually as well as financially. That team's togetherness is well known around the National Football League. Coach George Allen is the rah-rah type, a throwback to the old "win-one-for-The Gipper" days, a man who believes that emotional preparedness is nearly as important as the physical strength of the team.

There are George Allen detractors who disdain his methods and discount them as so much useless garbage. "I know some people figure that's all a bunch of high school stuff," said Moseley, "but I can tell you that it works. The Redskins are really a together-type of team. We have unity. When I came to the club, I had my train back on the right tracks. I had learned the hard way that only through Jesus Christ could I have the right kind of life here on earth and the expectatoin of a life after death. Going to the Redskins was a tremendous lift, too, and not just because I was joining a contending team. There are a lot of powerful Christians on that football squad.

"Growing up in the Central Baptist Church in Livingston, I was exposed to religion, but I did not allow myself to embrace Christianity. I finally realized that those setbacks—the divorce, the ups and downs in football—were God's way of trying to tell me something. He was making me sit up and pay attention. It took some doing, but he finally got through to me. I had to be hit over the head with God's hammer, and I went to my knees and prayed to him to deliver me. And he did just that.

"Sharon and I talked about it and prayed about it. We agreed we had to get involved with God and become active in church. One of the things that really influenced me was a Christian leadership conference. When we came back from that three-day conference, we were changed people. We could see things clearly. We could pray together, confront our problems, and find solutions through God's Word. And we went from a run-of-the-mill marriage to a good one, because we had a new dimension to our lives.

"We still find ourselves falling short of what we ought to be.

But now I try to be a good witness. That's why being with the Redskins presents such a wonderful chance for that sort of witnessing. We have some strong believers on the team. Our chapel leader, Tom Skinner, has become as much a part of our squad as any player (so much so that the Redskins pay his expenses to travel with the club as its official chaplain), and we draw strength from one another. Coach Allen recognizes Tom's importance to the team and believes in what we're accomplishing. I'm sure it makes us a better team on the field as well as better human beings off the field.

"As for myself, I'm a changed person. I'm happier. I'm better able to handle life's problems. I find myself better able to cope. And I think I'm becoming less self-centered. I try to look at the other person's side of things. When I pray now, I ask God to give me more insight and understanding. We live at a time when people are running away from reality and trying to escape it. But being a Christian means you can face up to the realities, even though they're harsh sometimes. A Christian can take lumps better than a non-believer. Like I said, it took a while for it all to sink into my head, but when I could not stand alone, all I had to do was ask him to stand with me. I can lose all else in life, but I can always have Jesus Christ."

24

The Man with the Good Medicine

In most sports organizations, the term "Doc" can mean medical doctor, trainer, physical therapist, or the custodian of the tape.

Around the National Football League there is but one "Doc" and the only medicine he dispenses could be called the best soul food in the world. The "doctor" part of it is strictly honorary.

Unlike most doctors, he makes house calls, works weekends, and charges nothing for his services. On the contrary, he pays his own expenses to visit his patients, but on the other hand he never has to worry about malpractice suits.

His name is Ira Lee Eshleman and he is the self-ordained chaplain to the National Football League, its twenty-eight teams, and hundreds of players who play the game for fun and profit. For nine years, Ira Lee Eshleman has carried on—almost single-handedly—his missionary work to the professional football player. It is largely through his efforts that every team in professional football, both in the United States and Canada, now includes a chapel service as a part of its pre-game routine. It is as much a part of the pro ritual as the taping of ankles and the studying of the play book and the game plan.

Doc Eshleman is likely to spend his Thanksgivings in Michigan because the Detroit Lions always play at home on Thanksgiving Day, and he wants to be certain the Lions and their opponents pause and give thanks. Wherever professional football players gather for the Super Bowl or the Pro Bowl, Doc Eshleman will be there as soon as the players begin to congregate. He'll seek out the coaches and make certain time is set aside for chapel services. Every weekend, from August through the final whistle of the Pro Bowl, Ira Lee Eshleman is on the road, trying to round up souls.

"All I'm trying to do," he said, "is answer a need and fulfill a promise I made to God."

That promise came back in 1967. Eshleman had retired after many extraordinarily successful years as president and founder of the famed Bibletown U. S. A. center in Boca Raton, Florida. Even though only fifty years old, he was in constant pain from a pinched radial nerve.

"I was praying for God to deliver me from this ailment," he said. "I asked God to heal me, then to give me some definite indication what he wanted me to do with the rest of my life."

The answers began to take shape as Doc Eshleman took a group of people on a chartered plane to Puerto Rico to hear Dr. Billy Graham. On the trip were a couple of outstanding football players who had made strong commitments to Jesus Christ. During conversations with Don Shinnick and Raymond Berry, the idea of a chapel service for professional football teams cropped up. Some months later, Eshleman spoke with the then coach of the Atlanta Falcons, Norb Hecker, to see if there would be any objection to such a service. Hecker's reply was that he had no objection if that's what the players wanted. Seventeen Falcons showed up for the first service, and even though Eshleman did not know it at the time, he was launching a program that was to snowball to every city in the NFL and the Canadian Football League.

"I ran into Otto Graham and he suggested I come up to Washington and hold a similar service for the Washington Redskins," said Doc, "and we had twenty-six players turn out. I thought perhaps at the time God was giving me some indication of what he wanted me to do."

After that first service in Washington, seven players spoke privately with Eshleman and expressed a desire to know more about an intimate relationship with God. And while on a trip to Detroit a player confided to Doc that he had gone to church all his life but up to then had no real relationship with Jesus Christ.

"I pretty well knew right then we were on our way," Eshleman recalled. "It was a radical change for me—I had been accustomed to speaking before audiences of a thousand or more, and here I was in hotel rooms huddled with just an intimate group of players."

Eshleman met with some resistance.

"It was like walking on eggs for a while," he said, "and even now we have some apprehension from certain people. The National Football League is so well organized and so well run that anytime there is anything new, there is a certain amount of—well, let's call it suspicion. A new face around causes some eyebrows to be raised and some questions to be asked. It wasn't going to be easy to establish my own credibility. Let's face it— I was a stranger, starting to talk with players in hotel lobbies and outside of locker rooms. Coaches and management people dont' want anyone to be a distraction for the players. They have to focus full steam on the challenges of the game. I'd have to be candid and say that there were times when I did not feel I was being whole-heartedly welcomed by coaches and management."

Today, only one team in the National Football League discourages Doc Eshleman from taking an active part in the chapel service. That team has a rule that chapel services are okay, but that they must be run by the players themselves. Said Eshleman: "We had just organized a chapel service on this one team and I was talking with some of the players in the hotel lobby on the Saturday night before a game. The coach and the owner watched for a while, and finally asked one of the players who I was, and what was going on. The player explained about the chapel service and my part in it. He was told the club didn't want any outsiders involved in such a program. The player was in the process of explaining that he had personally asked me to come from Florida to New Orleans—and that I had paid my own way—then someone called and told me there had been a terrible plane crash in West Virginia, and that many members of the Marshall University football team had been killed. I was asked to come up there and set up a chapel service for the families. So within half an hour, I was on a plane headed for Huntington, West Virginia, to do what I could in that situation."

Today, Doc Eshleman tries to operate in just about the same way. Rarely does he follow a set pattern in his visits to the professional teams. He tries to see each club at least once during the season, but frequently will alter his plans if he gets a call from a player who needs individual counseling.

"Every time I speak to these athletes, I try to stress four great principles that I believe are the heartbeat or the good news of God: God loves us, and he has a plan for our lives and cares what happens to us. I tell the pro athlete that God did not make him like a worm to be trampled or like a leaf that falls to the ground. God set eternity in his heart. When Jesus Christ came, he came to put the joy of life into his heart.

"I tell them that all of us have sinned and come short of the glory of God. This thing called sin has separated them from God. Sin causes man to push God out into the perimeter of life, and man wants to run things himself. That's why man does what he does, because of the distance from which he operates from God. We believe that God built a bridge across the great gulf that separates man from God. That bridge is Jesus Christ. I try to make it very clear to these men that God came down and focused himself in the person of Jesus Christ, who went into the place of death to make full payment for the sins of the world. And that includes every man's sin."

Doc continues, "If we're reaching the professional football player, it's because we try to do it in an uncomplicated, sincere way. We just tell him that God loves him and has a plan for his life, that by nature man is sinful and therefore separated from God, that God made provision for sin in the person of Jesus Christ who was crucified and buried and who rose from the dead and who is coming again, and finally, that Jesus comes into one's life only by invitation."

Eshleman counts more than a hundred pro football players who have professed a faith in Jesus Christ in his nine years of ministry.

None of this would have happened, had it not been for an old missionary who came to a church near Lancaster, Pennsylvania, and laid it on the line to a church full of professing Christians about their sinful ways. Eshleman recalls how it happened:

"I had professed a faith in God at the age of twelve and joined the United Brethren Church near Millersville, Pennsylvania. Someone had come up to me and asked if I believed in Jesus Christ. I thought that was kind of silly since we celebrated his birthday and dated our calendars from his death. So I accepted Jesus Christ, but it was more intellectual assent to his existence than anything else. And I continued that way for nine years, with no real understanding that Christ died for me."

In the meantime, Ira Lee Eshleman finished his high school work—well ahead of most of the other students in that Pennsylvania Dutch country—went to work in a silk mill at Columbia, Pennsylvania, for six dollars a week and later got a job with the company building a dam about ten miles from his home.

He was twenty-one when he went to hear a missionary who had just returned from China. "He was the first preacher who ever got through to me," said Doc. "He got to me because he was speaking honestly. He challenged everyone in the audience, telling us that we were singing more lies than we were telling: 'You're singing words that say you will surrender all to him, but you know that's a lie because some of you haven't even surrendered 10 percent of what he has given you. Let's come clean and be truthful about what we are.'

"Well, driving home that night, I admitted to myself that I was one of those who quickly would forget all about what the preacher had said. But on a sudden impulse I turned my car off the road and stopped and prayed. After a few minutes I wheeled around and went back to see this man and told him I'd go to China if that's where God wanted me to go. I told him I'd give my company notice and be ready to leave in two weeks. He asked me what training I had for such a venture, and I told him I had memorized a hundred and fifty verses of Scripture. He suggested that I might need a little more training. But I was convinced right then and there that I wanted to totally give my life to Jesus Christ."

Ira Lee Eshleman began to make preparations to attend Moody Bible Institute in Chicago. It was there he met Viola Anderson. They were married, and when Ira Lee graduated as an ordained minister they were offered four churches.

"We decided to take the church that offered the least amount of money. I wanted to satisfy myself that we didn't go into the ministry for any reason other than to serve God."

The Eshlemans stayed at the Conley Memorial Baptist Church in Highland Park, on the outskirts of Detroit, Michigan, for five years.

"We took our vacations in Fort Lauderdale, Florida, for several years," he said, "and decided to go there full time and see if we could do some good in that area. We began a radio Bible-teaching ministry in four different cities—Miami, Fort Lauderdale, West Palm Beach, and Hollywood. Finally the radio ministry grew to include seventeen stations."

Then came the opportunity to set up a Bible conference in Florida. "It was the fourth time in my ministry I had written out the last dollar in our check book," he recalled. "We made a deposit on an abandoned radar base. Everyone was saying the Gold Coast area offered nothing but dog tracks, horse racing, jai alai, and night clubs. I believed we could put the voice of God down in that area."

What developed over the years was Bibletown U. S. A., the largest winter Bible conference center in America. The Bible conferences and the sacred concerts staged at Bibletown are known the world over. The largest of three auditoriums seats more than twenty-four hundred persons. It is a 300-acre complex that includes six hundred homes.

Along the way, Ira Lee and Viola were bringing up four children—Paul, Bonnie Jean, Dennis Lee, and Sharon Rose. Paul is assistant to Dr. Bill Bright in the widely acclaimed Campus Crusade work.

Then, in 1967, his health threatened, Ira Lee Eshleman prayed for new direction, a new mission field, and found pro football. "At the outset I believe I was the only person spending full time working with professional athletes, trying to introduce them to Jesus Christ. But it has grown far beyond my wildest expectations. Now there must be seven or eight people working full-time with the professional athletes. Now, I see an even greater work down the road. Naturally, we must continue to win the athletes into a positive relationship with Christ—but we're on the threshold of something really stimulating and far-reaching, and that is to make it possible for the Christian athlete to take his message into the crossroads of our population centers, and in turn use his faith and his testimony to win others to Christ. The Christian athlete, by sounding off with the wondrous message of how he solved the emptiness of his own life and found solutions to the nagging problems he faced, can work magic all across the nation.

"People will listen to these pros. They have a way of getting into places, and a way of opening doors that are closed to other people. It all goes back to the business of being accepted, the matter of being a hero in the eyes of the world. Well over seventy-five million people watch these men do their thing in the Super Bowl. Advertisers pay over $200,000 a minute for their commercial messages, so the impact is terrifyingly great. The pro athlete is a hero to young America—but he's a hero to old America as well."

Doc Eshleman's home base now is called Sports World Chaplaincy. He has a well organized plan now for a vast witnessing ministry. Here's how Doc Eshleman sees the prgoram:

"One hundred Christian athletes would fan out all over the country in the off-season and touch every part of society. We'd hit the high schools, the colleges, the churches, the marketplace.

These men would be prepared for this work through our post-season seminars and through learning sessions at our place in Florida or at our farm in the hills of Tennessee so they'd be ready to meet people and talk about Jesus Christ and what he's done in their lives.

"It'd be a sixteen-week program of evangelism throughout the country. The way we see it is that the athlete would work largely within a 150-mile radius of his home base, and since we have NFL teams all over the country with more on the way, we could cover the entire nation. We'd concentrate on three-day missions. On Friday the three-man evangelistic team would be in the high schools and universities. Saturday we'd arrange a civic get-together, perhaps jointly-sponsored by the local chamber of commerce. Saturday night is country club night, where we'd take the message to the executive sportsman, and show him how he could enrich his life through knowledge of Jesus Christ. Then on Sunday, we'd appear in two churches who'd be responsible for hosting the mission program in that particular city."

Eshleman said the players themselves suggested such a nationwide missionary undertaking.

At age sixty when most men are thinking of that comfortable retirement retreat, Ira Eshleman is going to his knees again, asking God for direction for still another ministry. Doc Eshleman is convinced that God offers the only good medicine for a sick world.

Acknowledgments

In the course of putting together this book, I spent a great deal of time with men who, in most quarters, are considered to be larger than life. They are men who do deeds that most men only dream about; they are men through whom others live, vicariously.

Although I have been involved with professional football for twenty years as a writer and broadcaster, I found I knew precious little about the men themselves. They have the same triumphs and tragedies, the same thrills and agonies as other men. Only because theirs is such a fishbowl existence are their peaks and valleys so magnified. I am grateful to these men, not only for the entertainment they provide and the professionalism they exhibit, but because they opened up their minds and hearts and spoke candidly about the most meaningful things in their world. I am stronger because of their sharing.

I am grateful to Pete Rozelle, the commissioner of the National Football League, and the members of his staff, and to the member teams of the NFL for their cooperation. Special thanks, too, is due John Carrara, Charles Pomeroy, Ralph Zundel, and Lawrence Grant who preached wonderful sermons in the First Baptist Church at Middleport, Ohio. Mostly, though, I am grateful to the late Lucille and Lisle Diles, who lived their sermons and who, by precept and example, showed Lois, Phyllis, Bill, Marge, and me what it is like to be a Christian.

DAVE DILES